ETHICAL HACKING: A HANDS-ON GUIDE FOR BEGINNERS

Learn the Art of Penetration Testing and Cybersecurity

THOMPSON CARTER

CONTENTS

INTRODUCTION 5

THE GROWING NEED FOR CYBERSECURITY 6
LEGAL AND ETHICAL BOUNDARIES 7
WHO IS THIS BOOK FOR? 7
HOW TO USE THIS BOOK 8
BRIEF CHAPTER OVERVIEW 9
CHAPTER 1: FOUNDATIONS OF CYBERSECURITY 11
CHAPTER 2: TYPES OF HACKERS AND THEIR MOTIVATIONS 19
CHAPTER 3: LEGAL ASPECTS OF ETHICAL HACKING 25
CHAPTER 4: SETTING UP A SAFE HACKING ENVIRONMENT 34
CHAPTER 5: NETWORKING BASICS FOR ETHICAL HACKERS 45
CHAPTER 6: OPERATING SYSTEMS ESSENTIALS (LINUX AND
WINDOWS) 55
CHAPTER 7: UNDERSTANDING VULNERABILITIES AND EXPLOITS ...65
CHAPTER 8: RECONNAISSANCE TECHNIQUES (FOOT PRINTING AND
SCANNING) 76
CHAPTER 9: SOCIAL ENGINEERING AND HUMAN VULNERABILITIES
.... 87
CHAPTER 10: GAINING INITIAL ACCESS (BREAKING INTO SYSTEMS) 98
CHAPTER 11: EXPLOITATION AND PRIVILEGE ESCALATION 108
CHAPTER 12: WIRELESS NETWORK HACKING 118
CHAPTER 13: WEB APPLICATION HACKING 130
CHAPTER 14: EXPLOITING DATABASES AND SQL INJECTION 141
CHAPTER 15: MALWARE BASICS AND COUNTERMEASURES 153
CHAPTER 16: NETWORK SNIFFING AND TRAFFIC ANALYSIS............ 165

CHAPTER 17: INTRODUCTION TO PENETRATION TESTING 177

CHAPTER 18: REPORTING AND DOCUMENTING VULNERABILITIES 188

CHAPTER 19: POST-EXPLOITATION AND COVERING TRACKS.......... 199

CHAPTER 20: ETHICAL HACKING TOOLS AND FRAMEWORKS 210

CHAPTER 21: CASE STUDIES AND REAL-WORLD APPLICATIONS 222

CHAPTER 22: BUILDING A CAREER IN ETHICAL HACKING.............. 233

INTRODUCTION

Understanding Ethical Hacking and Its Importance

In a world where data is as valuable as gold, safeguarding information is essential. Cyberattacks have surged over the years, impacting everyone from small businesses to global corporations and even governments. Ethical hacking, often called "white-hat" hacking, has emerged as a critical field within cybersecurity, dedicated to protecting these organizations from malicious attacks. Ethical hacking helps secure systems by identifying vulnerabilities before bad actors, or "black-hat" hackers, can exploit them. This introduction explores what ethical hacking is, its significance, and how this book serves as a guide to understanding and practicing it.

What is Ethical Hacking?

Ethical hacking is a proactive approach to cybersecurity where authorized professionals—known as ethical hackers—identify, test, and fix vulnerabilities within a system. Unlike malicious hacking, where hackers break into systems without permission to steal data or cause harm, ethical hackers are authorized to assess security levels, helping organizations bolster their defenses. Ethical hacking operates within legal boundaries, following strict guidelines to ensure that all actions are conducted responsibly, transparently, and with the full consent of the system owners.

Think of ethical hackers as security auditors for the digital realm. Just as physical buildings have locks, alarms, and security guards, digital systems need ethical hackers to test and ensure the strength of their defenses. These "white-hat" hackers use the same skills and techniques as their malicious counterparts, but their purpose is prevention and protection, not exploitation.

The Growing Need for Cybersecurity

In recent years, the frequency and scale of data breaches have shown why cybersecurity is vital. Major companies like Yahoo, Equifax, and even government entities have faced data breaches, with millions of records exposed. In each case, these breaches caused financial damage, eroded public trust, and highlighted the need for robust cybersecurity measures. Many of these incidents were preventable had the organizations taken proactive security measures.

For instance, in 2017, the Equifax data breach exposed the personal information of 147 million people. This breach could have been avoided if the company had patched a known vulnerability. Ethical hackers are instrumental in preventing such breaches by discovering weak points in a system's infrastructure before attackers do. As companies increasingly adopt digital solutions, ethical hackers are needed to protect these systems from potential threats.

Legal and Ethical Boundaries

Ethical hacking is governed by laws, codes of conduct, and industry certifications to ensure that security assessments are conducted responsibly. The legality of ethical hacking hinges on consent: ethical hackers must have explicit permission from system owners to test and analyze systems. The Computer Fraud and Abuse Act (CFAA) in the United States, for example, outlines the boundaries of legal access to computer systems. Without authorization, hacking—no matter the intent—is illegal and punishable by law.

Certifications such as the Certified Ethical Hacker (CEH), Offensive Security Certified Professional (OSCP), and CompTIA Security+ provide ethical hackers with credentials that demonstrate their skills and commitment to ethical standards. These certifications require individuals to undergo training and testing, ensuring that they possess the knowledge needed to perform security assessments ethically and legally.

Who is This Book For?

This book is tailored for anyone interested in understanding and applying ethical hacking principles. It is accessible to beginners with little to no prior experience in cybersecurity, making it suitable for IT enthusiasts, students, and aspiring security professionals alike. Whether you're exploring cybersecurity as a career or want to gain practical skills to secure your personal or organizational systems, this book is a step-by-step guide to ethical hacking fundamentals.

This hands-on guide will take you through the basics, teach you the tools and techniques used by professionals, and give you practical scenarios to apply your knowledge. By the end, you'll have a solid foundation in ethical hacking and be equipped with essential skills that are both valuable and in demand.

How to Use This Book

This book encourages a hands-on, practice-based approach to ethical hacking. Readers are advised to set up a secure lab environment using virtual machines (VMs) to safely experiment with the concepts presented. Tools like VirtualBox or VMware allow you to create isolated environments where you can practice hacking techniques without affecting real systems.

Each chapter will introduce new concepts, followed by exercises or examples that let you apply what you've learned. Ethical hacking isn't a purely theoretical field; the best way to understand it is through active engagement and experimentation. Follow the exercises and suggestions for setting up labs to get the most out of this book.

Brief Chapter Overview

This book is organized into 22 chapters, each building on the previous ones to create a cohesive learning journey. Starting with the basics of cybersecurity and networking, we will progress through increasingly complex techniques and tools used by ethical hackers. Here's a quick breakdown:

- Chapter 1-3: Foundational concepts in cybersecurity, types of hackers, and the legal and ethical framework that governs ethical hacking.
- Chapters 4-7: Setting up a secure lab, basic networking, and operating system essentials (Linux and Windows).
- Chapters 8-11: Exploring reconnaissance, social engineering, and gaining initial access to systems.
- Chapters 12-17: Advanced techniques like exploitation, privilege escalation, wireless network hacking, web application vulnerabilities, and malware basics.
- Chapters 18-21: Conducting penetration tests, documenting findings, covering tracks, and tools and frameworks used in ethical hacking.
- Chapter 22: Building a career in ethical hacking, covering certifications, job roles, and career advice.

By the end of this journey, you'll understand how to conduct a security assessment ethically and be well-equipped to pursue further studies or a career in ethical hacking.

This book is designed to make ethical hacking accessible, relatable, and engaging for beginners. Ready to dive in? Let's start building your skills step-by-step, laying the foundation for a responsible and impactful career in ethical hacking.

CHAPTER 1: FOUNDATIONS OF CYBERSECURITY

In today's digital age, cybersecurity forms the backbone of personal, corporate, and governmental safety. With so much sensitive information stored and transmitted digitally, understanding cybersecurity principles is essential not only for professionals but also for individuals who want to protect their data and systems. This chapter introduces foundational cybersecurity concepts, starting with core principles, and provides real-world examples to illustrate why these principles are critical.

Why Cybersecurity Matters

Cybersecurity is the practice of defending computers, networks, and data from malicious attacks. In recent years, cyber threats have escalated, both in frequency and sophistication. Cybersecurity breaches can result in data loss, financial damages, reputational harm, and, in severe cases, national security risks.

Imagine a world without cybersecurity—where financial records, personal information, and government data could be accessed by anyone, at any time. Businesses could lose their trade secrets, individuals could suffer identity theft, and governments could face espionage. Cybersecurity seeks to protect against these threats, and at its core are three key principles: confidentiality, integrity, and availability, commonly referred to as the CIA Triad.

The CIA Triad: Core Principles of Cybersecurity

The CIA Triad is the foundation of cybersecurity, encapsulating the essential principles that guide how information and systems should be protected:

1. **Confidentiality**

   - **Definition**: Ensures that sensitive information is only accessible to those who are authorized to view it.

   - **Example**: When you log into your bank account online, confidentiality ensures that only you and the bank can view your account information.

   - **Importance**: Breaches of confidentiality, such as unauthorized access to private emails or data leaks, can lead to identity theft, financial fraud, or the exposure of sensitive business information.

2. Integrity

- o **Definition**: Ensures that information is accurate and has not been altered by unauthorized individuals.

- o **Example**: Imagine a medical record system where patient data can only be modified by authorized medical staff. Integrity ensures that the data remains correct, preventing harmful changes.

- o **Importance**: Integrity is essential for maintaining trust in systems. If a company's financial records or an individual's health records can be modified by anyone, the reliability and credibility of that information would be compromised.

3. Availability

- o **Definition**: Ensures that information and resources are accessible when needed by authorized users.

- o **Example**: Availability means that your email server is up and running, allowing you to check your messages anytime.

- o **Importance**: If systems and data are not available when needed, businesses can lose money, productivity can drop, and essential services may be disrupted. An example of a common threat to availability is a Distributed Denial of Service (DDoS) attack, which overwhelms systems to make them unavailable to users.

Real-World Examples: Cybersecurity Breaches and Attack Techniques

To fully understand the importance of cybersecurity, let's look at some notable cyberattacks and how they targeted aspects of the CIA Triad:

1. **Confidentiality Breach: Yahoo Data Breach (2013-2014)**

   - o **What Happened**: Over 3 billion Yahoo user accounts were compromised, exposing personal information such as names, email addresses, and hashed passwords.

   - o **Impact**: The breach exposed sensitive information and demonstrated how a lack of robust security protocols can lead to massive confidentiality losses.

- o **Lessons Learned**: Organizations must implement stringent access controls, encryption methods, and regular audits to protect user data confidentiality.

2. **Integrity Attack: Stuxnet Worm (2010)**

- o **What Happened**: Stuxnet, a highly sophisticated computer worm, targeted Iran's nuclear program by infiltrating industrial control systems and subtly altering their functioning, while reporting false information to monitoring systems.

- o **Impact**: By tampering with the integrity of system data and processes, Stuxnet disrupted operations without immediate detection, setting a powerful example of how integrity breaches can cause physical and operational damage.

- o **Lessons Learned**: Monitoring system logs and implementing integrity checks can help detect unusual behavior and protect critical infrastructure from similar attacks.

3. **Availability Attack: Dyn DDoS Attack (2016)**

   o **What Happened**: A massive DDoS attack targeted Dyn, a company that provides domain name services, disrupting internet access across major websites like Twitter, Netflix, and Spotify.

   o **Impact**: By overwhelming the DNS servers with traffic, attackers rendered these services temporarily unavailable, highlighting vulnerabilities in internet infrastructure.

   o **Lessons Learned**: Building redundancy, implementing DDoS mitigation tools, and distributing critical services across multiple locations can help maintain availability and prevent such attacks.

Understanding Vulnerabilities and Exploitation Basics

Each cyberattack exploits a vulnerability in the system—whether it's weak password management, software flaws, or unprotected data. These vulnerabilities can be classified into various categories:

1. **Software Vulnerabilities**

- o Bugs or flaws in software code can allow attackers to bypass security measures. For instance, the famous Heartbleed vulnerability in the OpenSSL library allowed attackers to read data from secure communications.

2. **Human Vulnerabilities**

- o Human error, such as clicking on phishing links, weak password usage, and failure to follow security protocols, remains one of the most common causes of cybersecurity breaches.

3. **Network Vulnerabilities**

- o Poorly configured networks, open ports, and outdated systems can expose networked devices to attackers. Network vulnerabilities are often exploited to gain unauthorized access or launch DDoS attacks.

Understanding the types of vulnerabilities and how attackers exploit them is essential for ethical hackers, as it helps them think like attackers to identify and close potential security gaps.

Cybersecurity principles are the building blocks for anyone aiming to understand or work in cybersecurity. The CIA

Triad—confidentiality, integrity, and availability—serves as a compass guiding all security efforts. By learning from real-world breaches, we can see the devastating effects that occur when these principles are compromised.

This chapter provided a foundation for understanding cybersecurity's purpose and principles. As we progress through the book, you'll see how these principles apply in practice as we delve into more specific techniques, tools, and hands-on methods for ethical hacking. By grasping the importance of these fundamental concepts, you're preparing to engage thoughtfully and responsibly with the field of cybersecurity.

CHAPTER 2: TYPES OF HACKERS AND THEIR MOTIVATIONS

In the cybersecurity world, hackers play various roles, each with distinct motivations, methods, and ethical boundaries. While the term "hacker" often evokes images of someone with malicious intent, not all hackers are alike. Hackers are often classified into three main types based on their intent and behavior: white-hat, black-hat, and gray-hat hackers. Understanding these distinctions is critical for ethical hackers, as it helps clarify the motivations that separate ethical hacking from malicious hacking. This chapter breaks down these three types and provides historical examples that highlight their unique traits and why ethical hacking (white-hat hacking) stands out.

White-Hat Hackers (Ethical Hackers)

White-hat hackers, or ethical hackers, work with organizations to improve security by identifying and addressing vulnerabilities in systems, networks, and applications. Their goal is to protect data and systems from potential breaches and attacks. Unlike other hackers, white-hats operate within legal and ethical boundaries, only accessing systems with permission. They adhere to codes of conduct, industry regulations, and often hold certifications, such as the Certified Ethical Hacker (CEH) or Offensive Security Certified Professional (OSCP), which affirm their commitment to ethical standards and practices.

Key Characteristics of White-Hat Hackers:

- **Authorization**: White-hat hackers always have permission from the system owner to conduct tests.

- **Methodology**: They follow strict ethical guidelines, conduct thorough assessments, and report findings to system owners.

- **Purpose**: Their main goal is to improve security and prevent unauthorized access by malicious actors.

Historical Example: Google's Bug Bounty Program

In 2010, Google launched one of the first large-scale bug bounty programs, encouraging ethical hackers to find and report security vulnerabilities in its systems. By offering monetary rewards, Google incentivized white-hat hackers to disclose vulnerabilities responsibly, resulting in thousands of security improvements across products like Chrome, Gmail, and Android. This program has become a standard in the industry, highlighting the positive impact of ethical hacking and demonstrating how it can contribute to the safety of widely used technologies.

Black-Hat Hackers (Malicious Hackers)

Black-hat hackers, often depicted as the "villains" of the cyber world, operate outside legal and ethical boundaries, seeking unauthorized access to systems for personal gain, revenge, or simply the thrill of hacking. These hackers may target individuals, businesses, or even government entities, often causing financial loss, reputational damage, or widespread disruption. Black-hat hacking activities include stealing data, spreading malware, deploying ransomware, and engaging in other forms of cybercrime.

Key Characteristics of Black-Hat Hackers:

- **Unauthorized Access**: Black-hat hackers break into systems without permission and often without the system owner's knowledge.

- **Malicious Intent**: Motivations often include financial gain, personal vendettas, or causing chaos.

- **Illegal Actions**: Black-hat hacking is illegal, and those caught can face severe penalties, including fines and prison sentences.

Historical Example: The 2017 Equifax Data Breach

In 2017, one of the largest data breaches in history occurred when black-hat hackers exploited a vulnerability in Equifax's systems, exposing the personal data of 147 million individuals. The breach included sensitive information such as social security numbers, addresses, and credit card details. This attack not only resulted in significant financial and reputational damage for Equifax but also raised public awareness of the consequences of neglecting cybersecurity. The Equifax breach is an example of the devastation black-hat hackers can cause by exploiting unpatched vulnerabilities.

Gray-Hat Hackers

Gray-hat hackers straddle the line between white-hat and black-hat hackers. They may access systems without permission but claim they do so to expose vulnerabilities for the greater good. Although gray-hat hackers do not typically have malicious intent, they still violate ethical and legal boundaries by acting without explicit authorization. Gray-hats may publicize vulnerabilities to pressure companies into making security improvements, often without waiting for a response from the affected organization.

Key Characteristics of Gray-Hat Hackers:

- **Mixed Intentions**: Gray-hats may act to highlight security flaws but often do so without authorization.

- **Questionable Ethics**: Their actions, though not necessarily malicious, can still lead to unintended consequences, such as making vulnerabilities public before they're fixed.

- **Illegality**: Since they operate without permission, gray-hat hacking is typically illegal, even if done with good intentions.

Historical Example: The Case of Adrian Lamo

Adrian Lamo, often described as a gray-hat hacker, became known for hacking into high-profile networks, including The New York Times, Microsoft, and Yahoo, in the early 2000s. Lamo did not steal or sell data but instead notified the companies of their security weaknesses, sometimes even helping to fix the issues. Despite his claims of goodwill, Lamo's actions were unauthorized, and he eventually faced legal consequences. His case is often cited as an example of how gray-hat hackers, despite good intentions, can still cross ethical and legal lines.

Why Ethical Hacking Stands Out

While black-hat and gray-hat hackers can cause harm through unauthorized access, ethical hackers serve a unique and valuable role in today's cybersecurity landscape. Organizations, governments, and businesses increasingly seek ethical hackers to protect their data and systems, recognizing the essential role these professionals play in proactive defense. By following strict guidelines, ethical hackers ensure that vulnerabilities are identified and addressed without causing harm or risking data breaches.

The Value of Ethical Hacking

1. **Proactive Defense**: Ethical hackers help prevent cyberattacks by identifying weaknesses before they're exploited.

2. **Transparency and Trust**: White-hat hackers operate openly and ethically, fostering trust between cybersecurity professionals and organizations.

3. **Legal and Ethical Standards**: White-hats follow the law, ensuring their actions support and reinforce cybersecurity measures rather than undermining them.

This chapter introduced the main types of hackers—white-hat, black-hat, and gray-hat—and explained their defining motivations and ethical boundaries. While black-hat hackers exploit systems maliciously and gray-hats operate in a gray area, ethical hackers stand apart by adhering to legal standards and a commitment to security improvement. The work of ethical hackers helps protect individuals, businesses, and governments, playing a critical role in today's cybersecurity landscape.

In the next chapter, we'll delve into the legal frameworks that govern ethical hacking, exploring how white-hat hackers can operate responsibly and within the boundaries of the law. This knowledge is essential for understanding the broader responsibilities of ethical hackers and navigating the ethical landscape of cybersecurity.

CHAPTER 3: LEGAL ASPECTS OF ETHICAL HACKING

Ethical hacking is a powerful tool for identifying and mitigating cybersecurity risks, but it must be conducted within the legal boundaries established by various laws and regulations. While ethical hackers work to protect systems, failing to follow legal procedures—even with good intentions—can lead to serious consequences. This chapter explores the legal framework governing ethical hacking, highlighting the importance of authorization and discussing key laws, such as the Computer Fraud and Abuse Act (CFAA), that shape the cybersecurity landscape.

Understanding the Legal Landscape of Ethical Hacking

Ethical hacking, or "white-hat" hacking, involves using hacking skills to find and fix vulnerabilities with the explicit permission of the system owner. Although ethical hackers work to strengthen security, the methods they use can look very similar to those of malicious hackers. Because of this, clear legal guidelines exist to distinguish between authorized security testing and illegal hacking. Without proper authorization, even well-meaning hacking efforts can be prosecuted as criminal activities.

Cybersecurity laws differ by country, but many common principles define what is acceptable. In the United States, for example, laws like the Computer Fraud and Abuse Act (CFAA) set out strict rules regarding computer access, data protection, and unauthorized actions. Other countries have their own sets of laws, but in all cases, gaining explicit permission is essential before any hacking activity can be conducted legally.

Key Laws Governing Ethical Hacking

1. Computer Fraud and Abuse Act (CFAA) (United States)

The Computer Fraud and Abuse Act (CFAA) is one of the most important laws governing ethical hacking in the United States. Originally enacted in 1986, the CFAA was designed to prevent unauthorized access to computers and to protect sensitive data from cybercrime. Over the years, it has been expanded to cover a wide range of activities, from data theft to hacking and fraud.

Under the CFAA, it is illegal to:

- Access a computer without authorization or exceed authorized access.

- Obtain sensitive information from government databases or financial institutions without permission.

- Engage in activities that could damage systems, including installing malware or disrupting network services.

While the CFAA aims to protect systems from malicious hackers, its broad language means that even well-intentioned actions can sometimes be prosecuted if they lack explicit authorization. For ethical hackers, this means they must secure clear, written permission from the system owner before conducting any testing to avoid violating the CFAA.

2. General Data Protection Regulation (GDPR) (European Union)

The GDPR, enacted by the European Union in 2018, primarily focuses on data protection and privacy. It governs how organizations collect, store, and manage personal data for individuals within the EU. While GDPR does not specifically target ethical hacking, it impacts cybersecurity practices by requiring organizations to implement adequate security measures to protect personal data.

Under the GDPR:

- Organizations must secure personal data and prevent unauthorized access.

- Data breaches must be reported within 72 hours of discovery.

- Non-compliance can lead to substantial fines, with penalties of up to 4% of global annual revenue.

For ethical hackers, GDPR means that any security testing involving personal data must be carefully handled to avoid privacy violations. It also underscores the importance of gaining permission, as unauthorized access to systems containing personal data could violate GDPR regulations.

3. UK Computer Misuse Act (CMA)

In the United Kingdom, the Computer Misuse Act (CMA) is the primary law governing computer security. Similar to the CFAA, the CMA prohibits unauthorized access to computer systems, unauthorized data modifications, and the creation or distribution of malicious software. The CMA makes it illegal to:

- Access data or systems without permission.

- Commit or facilitate criminal activities through unauthorized access.

- Intentionally damage data or system functionality, including actions like data deletion or malware deployment.

For ethical hackers, the CMA reinforces the necessity of authorization. Without clear consent, any hacking activity could be interpreted as a breach of the CMA, even if conducted with good intentions.

4. Payment Card Industry Data Security Standard (PCI-DSS)

PCI-DSS is a set of security standards, rather than a law, that regulates how companies must handle credit card data. This standard is mandatory for companies that process, store, or transmit credit card information. PCI-DSS mandates regular security testing, including penetration tests, to protect cardholder data.

Key PCI-DSS requirements:

- Conduct regular vulnerability scans and penetration tests.

- Protect stored cardholder data through encryption and secure storage.

- Implement strong access control measures, such as two-factor authentication.

Ethical hackers working with companies that handle credit card data must follow PCI-DSS requirements and ensure all security tests are authorized. PCI-DSS highlights the importance of regular security testing, which ethical hackers conduct to ensure compliance.

Importance of Gaining Authorization Before Testing Systems

Authorization is a foundational principle in ethical hacking. Without permission from the system owner, hacking—even for testing purposes—can be deemed illegal. Here's why authorization is critical:

1. **Legal Protection**

   o Gaining written authorization protects ethical hackers from legal consequences. Authorization clarifies that all activities are performed with the consent of the system owner, ensuring compliance with laws like the CFAA and CMA.

   o For penetration testers and consultants, a signed agreement outlining the scope of testing is essential. This "scope of work" document specifies which systems and activities are permitted, protecting the hacker and the client.

2. Respecting Ethical Boundaries

o   Ethical hacking is rooted in trust, transparency, and respect for boundaries. Authorization ensures that all actions align with the goals and ethical standards of cybersecurity.

o   Without authorization, ethical hacking could lead to unintended consequences, such as data exposure or service disruption. Authorization provides clear parameters, ensuring that testing does not disrupt business operations or jeopardize data privacy.

3. Establishing a Defined Scope of Testing

o   Authorization establishes the scope of testing, outlining which systems, networks, and applications are fair game. A defined scope prevents ethical hackers from unintentionally overstepping boundaries and testing areas that the client does not wish to include.

o   For instance, a company may want ethical hackers to focus on its internal network and exclude certain databases. Having a defined scope clarifies expectations and minimizes risk.

4. Mitigating Risks

- ○ Ethical hacking inherently involves risk, as testing can potentially expose vulnerabilities that could be exploited if not properly managed. Authorization includes risk mitigation strategies, such as outlining protocols in the event that a vulnerability is discovered.

- ○ It also clarifies how vulnerabilities should be reported, who should be notified, and the steps to ensure that identified issues are resolved securely.

Real-World Example: The Importance of Authorization

Case Study: The Marriott International Data Breach

In 2014, hackers breached Starwood Hotels, which was later acquired by Marriott International. Personal data of approximately 500 million customers was exposed, including credit card and passport information. The incident underscored the need for regular and authorized security testing, as well as clear data protection practices.

Following the breach, Marriott faced extensive investigations and penalties, including a fine of nearly $125 million by the UK's Information Commissioner's Office (ICO). This case highlights why gaining authorization for regular security assessments is critical for large organizations. With proper testing and authorization, companies can address vulnerabilities before they lead to data breaches and associated penalties.

Best Practices for Ethical Hackers: Staying Within Legal Boundaries

1. **Get Written Authorization**

   o Ensure that permission is obtained in writing, detailing the scope of work, timeframe, and specific testing activities. This document is legally protective and confirms that all actions are consensual.

2. **Define the Scope Clearly**

   o Specify the systems, networks, and areas covered by the assessment. Avoid "out-of-scope" systems to prevent unintended legal or operational issues.

3. **Keep Records and Logs**

   o Document all activities, findings, and interactions with the system. Detailed records provide accountability and can be used as evidence to show that actions were within the agreed scope.

4. **Report Findings Responsibly**

   o Ensure that vulnerabilities are reported only to authorized contacts. Avoid sharing findings with third parties, as unauthorized disclosure could violate privacy laws or data protection agreements.

5. **Follow Industry Standards and Certifications**

   o Following standards like PCI-DSS or obtaining certifications such as CEH or OSCP reinforces ethical commitment and demonstrates professionalism.

Ethical hacking is an effective way to identify and mitigate cybersecurity risks, but it must be conducted responsibly and within legal parameters. Laws like the Computer Fraud and Abuse Act, GDPR, and the Computer Misuse Act set essential boundaries for hacking activities. The key takeaway from this chapter is the importance of authorization: without explicit permission, ethical hackers risk legal consequences that could undermine their efforts to improve security.

By obtaining authorization, ethical hackers protect themselves and their clients, ensuring that their work supports safe, legal, and effective cybersecurity practices. In the next chapter, we'll look at how to set up a secure testing environment, discussing the tools and virtual machines that ethical hackers can use to practice safely without affecting live systems.

CHAPTER 4: SETTING UP A SAFE HACKING ENVIRONMENT

One of the first steps in learning and practicing ethical hacking is setting up a safe and secure environment to test your skills. Using real systems without authorization is illegal, so creating an isolated lab environment is essential for ethical hackers. This chapter will guide you through setting up a secure lab using virtual machines (VMs) and network simulators, providing a controlled space to explore hacking techniques without affecting live systems.

Why a Safe Hacking Environment is Essential

A safe lab environment allows ethical hackers to simulate real-world network scenarios and experiment with various tools without risking harm to actual systems or violating legal boundaries. By setting up a controlled lab, you can:

- **Safely Practice Skills**: Experiment with techniques and tools without worrying about causing real-world damage.

- **Understand Network Behavior**: Simulate network configurations to learn how systems interact, which is crucial for recognizing vulnerabilities.

- **Control and Isolate Testing**: Avoid affecting other networks or devices, protecting your data and keeping unauthorized access to a minimum.

- **Create Real-World Scenarios**: Use network simulators to build realistic environments, like a small corporate network, for hands-on testing.

Key Components for a Safe Hacking Lab

1. **Virtual Machines (VMs)**

   o Virtual machines are software emulations of physical computers that run on your own computer. Using virtualization software, you can run multiple VMs with different operating systems, such as Windows, Linux, or macOS, on a single host machine.

2. **Network Simulators**

   o Network simulators allow you to emulate complex network configurations without using physical hardware. They simulate routers, switches, and firewalls, letting you build detailed network environments and test network security setups.

3. **Penetration Testing Tools**

   o Ethical hacking relies on various tools to conduct vulnerability assessments, network scans, and exploit testing. In a safe lab, you'll be able to use tools like Nmap, Metasploit, Wireshark, and Burp Suite.

Choosing Virtualization Software

Virtualization software is at the core of your hacking lab setup. Two of the most popular options are **VirtualBox** and **VMware**. Both allow you to run multiple virtual machines, creating an environment where you can simulate networks and test security configurations.

1. VirtualBox

- **Developer**: Oracle

- **Cost**: Free (open source)

- **Features**:

    o Supports various operating systems, including Windows, Linux, macOS, and Solaris.

    o Easy-to-use interface suitable for beginners.

    o Snapshots feature allows you to save the VM state and revert if needed, which is useful for experimenting.

    o Network configuration options, allowing you to set up isolated networks for your VMs.

2. VMware Workstation and VMware Player

- **Developer**: VMware, Inc.

- **Cost**: VMware Workstation is paid; VMware Player is free for personal use.

- **Features**:

  ○ Robust and widely used in professional environments, offering high performance and advanced features.

  ○ Extensive support for snapshots and cloning, which can help when testing different scenarios.

  ○ Enhanced networking options that allow complex setups, such as creating multiple network adapters and virtual networks.

Recommendation: For beginners, VirtualBox is an excellent option due to its free availability and ease of use. However, if you're aiming for professional penetration testing, VMware Workstation is worth considering for its advanced features and compatibility with larger labs.

Setting Up Your Virtual Machines (VMs)

Once you've chosen your virtualization software, the next step is setting up virtual machines to simulate different operating systems. Having a mix of systems—such as Windows, Linux, and even specialized distributions like Kali Linux—will give you a well-rounded testing environment.

1. Download and Install the Virtualization Software

- Visit the VirtualBox or VMware website to download the software compatible with your operating system.

- Follow the installation instructions, which usually involve straightforward steps.

2. Download Operating System Images

- To create VMs, you'll need operating system images (ISO files). Common options for ethical hacking labs include:

  o **Kali Linux**: A Linux distribution designed for penetration testing, pre-installed with tools like Nmap, Metasploit, and Wireshark.

  o **Windows**: Windows OS is essential for testing vulnerabilities in widely used operating systems.

  o **Ubuntu or Other Linux Distributions**: Practicing on other Linux systems helps broaden your understanding of system diversity.

3. Create Virtual Machines

- Open your virtualization software and create a new VM.

- Assign CPU, memory, and storage based on your system's capacity. For a basic lab, 2GB of RAM per VM should be sufficient, though more will improve performance.

- Mount the OS ISO file to the VM and follow the installation steps for each OS.

4. Configure Networking in Virtual Machines

- Networking options vary by virtualization software, but here are common setups:

    o **NAT (Network Address Translation)**: Provides internet access but isolates the VM from other network devices. Ideal for basic setups.

    o **Host-Only Network**: Creates a private network between the host and VM, ideal for testing internal networks.

    o **Bridged Network**: Connects VMs to the same network as the host, useful for more advanced networking scenarios.

Using Network Simulators

Network simulators allow you to create detailed, complex network environments. Tools like Cisco Packet Tracer and GNS3 (Graphical Network Simulator-3) are popular options:

1. Cisco Packet Tracer

- **Cost**: Free for Cisco Networking Academy students; otherwise, limited free access.

- **Features**:

  o Simulates Cisco routers, switches, firewalls, and IoT devices.

  o Visual interface to design network topologies, ideal for beginners.

  o Useful for practicing network configurations, especially if studying for Cisco certifications.

2. GNS3

- **Cost**: Free (open source)

- **Features**:

  o Supports a wide range of devices and can integrate with VirtualBox and VMware VMs.

  o Used in professional environments for complex network simulations.

  o Allows you to configure advanced network setups and simulate real-world networking conditions, like router protocols and firewalls.

Recommendation: For beginners, Cisco Packet Tracer is a user-friendly option. GNS3 is more complex but excellent for advanced users who need to simulate detailed network environments.

Essential Tools for Your Lab Environment

In addition to setting up VMs and network simulators, certain tools are essential for practicing ethical hacking techniques. Many of these tools are pre-installed in Kali Linux:

1. Nmap (Network Mapper)

- **Purpose**: Network scanning and discovery.

- **Use**: Nmap identifies devices, services, and open ports on a network, which is essential for reconnaissance in ethical hacking.

2. Metasploit Framework

- **Purpose**: Exploitation framework.

- **Use**: Metasploit allows ethical hackers to test vulnerabilities by simulating attacks on target systems, helping assess their security.

3. Wireshark

- **Purpose**: Network packet analysis.

- **Use**: Wireshark captures and analyzes network traffic in real time, allowing ethical hackers to identify potential security issues or suspicious activity.

4. Burp Suite

- **Purpose**: Web application security testing.

- **Use**: Burp Suite is widely used for testing web applications, allowing ethical hackers to analyze and manipulate traffic between a browser and a web server.

Tip: As a beginner, focus on learning the basics of these tools. Kali Linux provides an excellent foundation with its pre-installed tools, which cover a wide range of tasks for ethical hacking.

Step-by-Step: Creating Your First Lab Setup

Here's a quick guide to setting up a basic lab environment with VirtualBox, a Kali Linux VM, and a Windows VM:

1. **Install VirtualBox**: Download VirtualBox from Oracle's website and install it on your computer.

2. **Download Kali Linux ISO**: Visit the Kali Linux website and download the latest ISO file.

3. **Create a New VM**:

    o Open VirtualBox, click "New," and name your VM "Kali Linux."

    o Set the OS type to "Linux" and the version to "Debian 64-bit."

    o Allocate 2GB RAM and 20GB disk space.

4. **Mount the ISO**:

    o Under "Storage," select the empty disk and add the Kali Linux ISO.

5. **Configure Networking**:

    o Choose "Host-Only" or "NAT" for networking to ensure isolation.

6. **Install Kali Linux**:

    o Start the VM and follow the installation instructions, configuring the system as needed.

7. **Repeat for Windows VM** (optional): Follow similar steps to install a Windows VM, using a Host-Only network to simulate internal network conditions.

Setting up a safe lab environment is an essential step in ethical hacking, providing a risk-free space to learn, experiment, and build cybersecurity skills. Virtual machines, network simulators, and essential tools create a powerful environment that mirrors real-world systems. By following these steps and practicing in a safe environment, you'll be better prepared to conduct ethical hacking activities legally and responsibly.

In the next chapter, we'll cover networking basics, exploring the protocols and configurations that ethical hackers need to understand to navigate networks and identify vulnerabilities. Networking knowledge is crucial for ethical hackers, as it forms the backbone of most systems they will assess.

CHAPTER 5: NETWORKING BASICS FOR ETHICAL HACKERS

Networking knowledge is foundational for ethical hackers. Understanding how networks and protocols operate allows you to identify potential vulnerabilities, navigate system configurations, and analyze data flows. In this chapter, we'll cover essential networking concepts and protocols, such as TCP/IP, DNS, and DHCP, and explain how an understanding of these elements aids in recognizing security weaknesses.

Understanding Networks and Their Components

A network is essentially a group of interconnected devices that share resources and information. These devices—like computers, servers, routers, and switches—communicate using specific protocols, which are standardized rules that define how data is transmitted across the network.

Key Components of a Network:

- **Hosts**: Computers and other devices connected to a network.

- **Routers and Switches**: Devices that direct data between networked devices.

- **Firewalls**: Security devices that monitor and filter incoming and outgoing network traffic.

- **Servers**: Dedicated systems providing services, such as file storage or web hosting, to other devices on the network.

As an ethical hacker, understanding these components and how they interact is crucial. Vulnerabilities can exist at any point in a network, and knowing the network's structure helps you map out potential attack paths and areas to test.

Introduction to Network Protocols

Network protocols are the rules that govern how data is transmitted, received, and interpreted across a network. By understanding common protocols, ethical hackers can identify vulnerabilities in how data is transmitted and potentially intercept, modify, or manipulate that data. Here are some of the fundamental protocols every ethical hacker should know:

1. TCP/IP (Transmission Control Protocol/Internet Protocol)

TCP/IP is the foundational protocol suite for the internet and most internal networks. It consists of multiple layers, each handling specific tasks. The TCP/IP model is divided into four layers:

- **Application Layer**: Manages application protocols like HTTP, FTP, and SMTP.

- **Transport Layer**: Handles data transmission between systems, primarily using TCP and UDP.

- **Internet Layer**: Manages data addressing and routing, using protocols like IP and ICMP.

- **Link Layer**: Governs data transmission over physical media like Ethernet.

Key Concepts in TCP/IP:

- **IP Addresses**: Unique addresses assigned to devices on a network. They identify devices, making communication possible.

- **TCP vs. UDP**: TCP ensures data reliability through connection-oriented communication, while UDP is faster but lacks reliability features, making it useful for time-sensitive applications.

Why TCP/IP Matters for Ethical Hackers: Understanding TCP/IP is essential because it allows you to see how data flows between devices. Many attacks, such as IP spoofing, SYN floods, and port scanning, target weaknesses in TCP/IP.

2. DNS (Domain Name System)

DNS is responsible for translating human-readable domain names (like www.example.com) into IP addresses that computers can use to locate resources. DNS servers store these mappings and make network navigation easier for users.

DNS Vulnerabilities:

- **DNS Spoofing**: Attackers trick the DNS server into directing users to a fake IP address, potentially leading users to a malicious site.

- **DNS Cache Poisoning**: Attackers insert false data into the DNS cache, causing incorrect mappings and potential data theft or redirection.

Why DNS Matters for Ethical Hackers: DNS is frequently targeted by attackers aiming to redirect traffic. Ethical hackers often analyze DNS settings to ensure they are properly configured and secure against such attacks.

3. DHCP (Dynamic Host Configuration Protocol)

DHCP automatically assigns IP addresses to devices on a network, enabling new devices to connect without manual configuration. DHCP servers dynamically allocate IP addresses, managing and recycling them as devices connect and disconnect.

DHCP Vulnerabilities:

- **DHCP Starvation**: Attackers flood the network with fake DHCP requests, exhausting available IP addresses and potentially disrupting network services.

- **Rogue DHCP Server**: Attackers set up an unauthorized DHCP server to assign incorrect IP configurations, redirecting traffic or enabling data capture.

Why DHCP Matters for Ethical Hackers: Misconfigured or unauthorized DHCP servers can expose a network to attacks. Ethical hackers check DHCP settings to ensure secure, controlled IP address assignment.

4. ARP (Address Resolution Protocol)

ARP is used to resolve IP addresses to MAC (Media Access Control) addresses, enabling devices to communicate within a local network. When a device needs to find the MAC address of another device, it sends an ARP request, which is answered by the target device with its MAC address.

ARP Vulnerabilities:

- **ARP Spoofing/Poisoning**: Attackers manipulate ARP tables, associating their MAC address with the IP of a legitimate device, enabling them to intercept or alter data.

Why ARP Matters for Ethical Hackers: ARP poisoning is a common attack method used in man-in-the-middle (MitM) attacks. Ethical hackers use tools like Wireshark to detect signs of ARP spoofing and ensure ARP tables are secure.

5. HTTP and HTTPS (HyperText Transfer Protocol / Secure)

HTTP is the protocol for transferring web pages, while HTTPS is its secure counterpart, using SSL/TLS encryption to protect data in transit. HTTPS prevents interception by encrypting the data exchanged between clients and web servers.

HTTP/HTTPS Vulnerabilities:

- **Man-in-the-Middle (MitM) Attacks**: Attackers can intercept data in HTTP connections, capturing or altering information.

- **SSL/TLS Vulnerabilities**: Weak encryption or misconfigured SSL/TLS certificates can leave HTTPS vulnerable.

Why HTTP/HTTPS Matter for Ethical Hackers: Many web-based attacks exploit HTTP weaknesses. Ethical hackers often test SSL/TLS configurations and monitor HTTP traffic to identify security risks.

How Understanding Network Protocols Helps Identify Vulnerabilities

Knowing how network protocols work is essential for spotting security gaps. Here's how protocol knowledge can reveal weaknesses:

1. Identifying Vulnerabilities through Protocol Behavior

- **Protocol Analysis**: By analyzing how data flows over a network, ethical hackers can identify protocol-specific vulnerabilities, such as unencrypted traffic over HTTP or weak SSL/TLS configurations in HTTPS.

- **Misconfiguration**: Misconfigured protocols can leave networks exposed. For example, an open TCP port could reveal a vulnerable service, and weak DNS settings might allow for DNS spoofing.

2. Detecting and Preventing Common Attacks

- **Network Scanning and Mapping**: Ethical hackers use tools like Nmap to identify open ports and services on target networks. Knowing which protocols operate on each port helps you understand what services might be vulnerable.

- **Traffic Monitoring**: Protocol analysis with tools like Wireshark enables ethical hackers to spot anomalies, such as ARP spoofing, suspicious DNS queries, or unauthorized DHCP requests.

3. Gaining Insight into System Weaknesses

- **Authentication Weaknesses**: Protocols like Telnet (which transmits data in plain text) can expose sensitive data, making them weak points in network security. Ethical hackers can identify insecure protocols and recommend alternatives, such as SSH (Secure Shell) over Telnet.

- **Encryption Standards**: Understanding the differences between HTTP and HTTPS allows ethical hackers to detect unencrypted data transfers and recommend HTTPS implementations.

Tools for Networking Analysis

Several tools can help ethical hackers analyze network protocols and identify potential security issues:

1. **Wireshark**

   o **Function**: Packet capture and analysis.

   o **Use**: Wireshark enables you to capture and inspect network packets, revealing the details of each protocol in use. It's a powerful tool for monitoring live network traffic, diagnosing issues, and identifying security weaknesses.

2. **Nmap (Network Mapper)**

   o **Function**: Network discovery and scanning.

   o **Use**: Nmap allows you to scan networks for open ports, services, and active hosts. By identifying which protocols are in use, you can analyze potential vulnerabilities in network services.

3. **Netcat**

   o **Function**: Network debugging and port scanning.

   o **Use**: Often referred to as the "Swiss Army knife" for networking, Netcat can perform a range of tasks, from simple port scans to setting up reverse shells. It's especially useful for testing network connections and communication protocols.

4. **tcpdump**

   o **Function**: Network packet capture.

   o **Use**: tcpdump is a command-line tool that captures and displays packet data. While similar to Wireshark, it's text-based and useful for analyzing network traffic at a granular level.

Tip: Start by using these tools to explore basic network traffic. Analyze packets, observe how protocols like DNS and TCP behave, and identify potential vulnerabilities. This hands-on approach will strengthen your understanding of network protocols.

Understanding network protocols is crucial for ethical hackers. By familiarizing yourself with protocols like TCP/IP, DNS, DHCP, and

HTTP/HTTPS, you gain the ability to identify misconfigurations, detect vulnerabilities, and anticipate common attacks. Protocol knowledge, combined with network analysis tools, forms the basis for evaluating network security and implementing effective defenses.

In the next chapter, we'll dive into operating systems and their role in ethical hacking. You'll learn the basics of Linux and Windows, two of the most widely used operating systems in cybersecurity, and see how they provide different challenges and opportunities in penetration testing.

CHAPTER 6: OPERATING SYSTEMS ESSENTIALS (LINUX AND WINDOWS)

Operating systems (OS) are the backbone of all digital systems, controlling hardware resources, managing files, and enabling users to interact with devices. Ethical hackers need a strong grasp of both Linux and Windows, as these are the most commonly targeted and used operating systems in cybersecurity. This chapter provides an overview of these two operating systems, focusing on command lines, file structures, and permission systems—critical aspects for any ethical hacker.

Why Operating System Knowledge is Important for Ethical Hackers

Understanding the fundamentals of operating systems is crucial because:

- **System Management**: Ethical hackers often interact with OS-level commands, file structures, and settings to identify and exploit potential vulnerabilities.

- **Platform-Specific Exploits**: Many vulnerabilities are OS-specific, meaning they exist in one OS but not another. Ethical hackers must understand the nuances of each system.

- **Forensic Analysis**: When investigating potential breaches, knowing how files, logs, and permissions work helps ethical hackers track activity and uncover unauthorized access.

Linux Basics for Ethical Hackers

Linux is a popular choice in cybersecurity due to its open-source nature, flexibility, and powerful command-line interface. **Kali Linux** is a specialized Linux distribution specifically designed for penetration testing and ethical hacking, pre-installed with numerous security tools like Nmap, Metasploit, and Wireshark.

1. Linux Command Line Basics

The Linux command line is a powerful tool that allows users to manage files, control processes, and interact with the system at a granular level. Some essential commands for ethical hackers include:

- **ls**: Lists files and directories.

- **cd**: Changes directories.

- **mkdir**: Creates a new directory.

- **rm**: Removes files or directories.

- **cp** and **mv**: Copy and move files or directories.

- **chmod**: Changes file permissions.

- **chown**: Changes file ownership.

- **ping** and **traceroute**: Test network connectivity and trace network paths.

- **sudo**: Executes a command with elevated privileges (root access).

Command-line proficiency in Linux is essential for ethical hackers, as it enables quick navigation, scripting for automation, and direct interaction with security tools.

2. Linux File Structure

The Linux file structure is hierarchical, beginning with the root directory (/) and containing essential directories for system management, configuration, and user data. Key directories include:

- **/home**: Contains personal files and directories for each user.

- **/etc**: Stores system configuration files, such as network settings and user account details.

- **/bin** and **/sbin**: Store essential system binaries and scripts.

- **/var**: Contains log files, which are crucial for forensic analysis and monitoring.

- **/tmp**: A temporary directory used for session-based files, which resets upon reboot.

Understanding Linux's directory structure allows ethical hackers to locate important files quickly, check logs for unauthorized access, and examine configuration files for vulnerabilities.

3. Linux Permission System

Linux permissions control access to files and directories, preventing unauthorized users from modifying system-critical files. Permissions are represented as three sets (owner, group, and others) with three access types (read, write, and execute).

Example of Linux file permissions: -rwxr-xr--

- **Owner**: rwx (read, write, execute)

- **Group**: r-x (read, execute)

- **Others**: r-- (read only)

Changing Permissions with chmod:

- To grant a file executable permission to the owner, you'd use: chmod u+x filename

- Ethical hackers use these permissions to control access and test privilege escalation vulnerabilities, where an unauthorized user might gain higher permissions.

Root (Superuser):

- The root user has unrestricted access to all files and commands. Many Linux vulnerabilities center around unauthorized root access, so ethical hackers often test to ensure that sensitive commands are restricted to authorized users.

Windows Basics for Ethical Hackers

While Linux is a popular OS in cybersecurity, Windows remains the most widely used OS globally, especially in enterprise environments. Ethical hackers need to understand Windows to identify vulnerabilities in networks, as Windows-based exploits are often a target in real-world attacks.

1. Windows Command Line Basics (CMD and PowerShell)

Windows offers two primary command-line interfaces: **Command Prompt (CMD)** and **PowerShell**. PowerShell is especially valuable for ethical hackers, as it provides advanced scripting capabilities and access to system management tasks.

Common Windows Commands:

- **dir**: Lists files and directories (similar to ls in Linux).

- **cd**: Changes directories.

- **mkdir**: Creates a new directory.

- **del**: Deletes files.

- **copy** and **move**: Copy and move files.

- **netstat**: Displays network connections, useful for monitoring open ports and connections.

- **ipconfig**: Shows network configuration details, such as IP address, subnet mask, and gateway.

- **Get-Process** (PowerShell): Lists running processes.

- **Get-Service** (PowerShell): Displays services and their status.

PowerShell for Scripting and Automation: PowerShell is particularly useful for ethical hackers as it enables advanced scripting for task automation and access to many administrative functions that CMD lacks. For example, you can use PowerShell to automate network scans, retrieve user information, or interact with the Windows registry.

2. Windows File Structure

The Windows file structure is also hierarchical but differs significantly from Linux. Key directories include:

- **C:\Users**: Contains user-specific directories, such as Documents, Downloads, and AppData.

- **C:\Windows**: Contains system files necessary for the OS to function, such as the registry, drivers, and DLL files.

- **C:\Program Files**: Contains installed application files.

- **C:\System32**: Stores critical system executables and libraries.

- **Registry**: Windows also uses a hierarchical database called the registry, where system settings and user configurations are stored. Ethical hackers often examine the registry for misconfigurations or clues about unauthorized access.

Familiarity with Windows' directory structure helps ethical hackers locate configuration files, analyze application settings, and access system logs for security assessments.

3. Windows Permission System

Windows permissions are managed through Access Control Lists (ACLs), which specify the permissions granted to each user or group for individual files, folders, and system objects. Permissions include:

- **Full Control**: Grants complete access to a file or folder.

- **Read and Execute**: Allows viewing and running files but not modifying them.

- **Write**: Allows modifying or deleting files.

Role of Administrator Accounts:

- Windows administrator accounts have full control over the system, similar to Linux's root user. Ethical hackers often assess whether standard users have excessive permissions or if privileged accounts are adequately protected.

Understanding User Account Control (UAC):

- UAC helps prevent unauthorized changes by prompting for administrator approval before executing sensitive actions. Ethical hackers assess UAC settings to ensure it's not bypassed or disabled, as improper UAC settings can lead to privilege escalation attacks.

Comparing Linux and Windows from a Security Perspective

While Linux and Windows have similar security mechanisms, their implementation differs, affecting how vulnerabilities are identified and exploited.

Feature	Linux	Windows
File Structure	Root-based file hierarchy	User-based file hierarchy
Command Line	Strong command-line culture, used extensively for system management	Command Prompt and PowerShell, with PowerShell offering extensive scripting capabilities
Permissions	Owner, group, others model	Access Control Lists (ACLs)

Feature	Linux	Windows
Superuser	Root user	Administrator with UAC
Common Tools	Pre-installed security tools (e.g., in Kali Linux)	Third-party security tools, as well as PowerShell modules

Each OS has its strengths and weaknesses from a security standpoint. For instance, Linux's open-source nature allows for flexibility but may expose configurations, while Windows' popularity makes it a frequent target for malware and exploits.

Practicing OS Essentials for Ethical Hacking

To strengthen your skills with operating systems as an ethical hacker, practice the following exercises:

1. **Linux Exercises**

   o Use chmod and chown to experiment with file permissions.

   o Explore directories with ls, cd, and find commands.

   o Use ps and kill to manage processes and understand privilege escalation risks.

2. **Windows Exercises**

- o Use PowerShell to retrieve network configurations (Get-NetIPAddress), monitor running processes (Get-Process), and explore the registry.

- o Experiment with creating and modifying user permissions in folders, and examine the impact on access control.

- o Investigate Windows services with PowerShell (Get-Service) to learn about potential security risks associated with misconfigured services.

Operating systems are the foundation of cybersecurity, and an ethical hacker's proficiency in both Linux and Windows is essential for effective security assessments. By mastering the command line, file structures, and permission systems of each OS, ethical hackers can confidently navigate different environments, understand common vulnerabilities, and implement security recommendations.

In the next chapter, we'll explore common vulnerabilities and exploits, diving into how ethical hackers identify and assess weaknesses in system configurations, network protocols, and applications. Understanding these vulnerabilities is essential for simulating real-world attacks safely and effectively.

Chapter 7: Understanding Vulnerabilities and Exploits

One of the core responsibilities of an ethical hacker is identifying and understanding vulnerabilities—weak points in a system that attackers can exploit. By recognizing these vulnerabilities, ethical hackers can help organizations fix potential weaknesses before they're targeted by malicious actors. This chapter explores the types of vulnerabilities commonly found in systems and applications, how exploits leverage these vulnerabilities, and why patching is crucial for maintaining security.

What Are Vulnerabilities?

A vulnerability is any flaw or weakness in a system's software, hardware, or configuration that could be exploited by an attacker to gain unauthorized access, compromise data integrity, or disrupt service availability. Vulnerabilities can arise from various factors, including programming errors, misconfigurations, and weak access controls.

Vulnerabilities are generally categorized into different types, depending on where they occur and how they're exploited. Understanding these categories helps ethical hackers assess risks, prioritize their efforts, and recommend appropriate mitigation measures.

Common Types of Vulnerabilities

1. **Buffer Overflows**

   o **Description**: A buffer overflow occurs when a program writes more data to a buffer (a memory storage area) than it can hold, causing data to "overflow" into adjacent memory areas.

   o **Impact**: Attackers can exploit buffer overflows to overwrite executable code in memory, potentially executing malicious code to gain control over a system.

   o **Example**: In the past, vulnerabilities in software like Microsoft Excel allowed attackers to craft malicious files that caused buffer overflows, which could be triggered when users opened the infected files.

2. **SQL Injection (SQLi)**

   o **Description**: SQL injection occurs when attackers insert malicious SQL code into input fields in web applications, causing the backend database to execute unauthorized commands.

   o **Impact**: Attackers can retrieve, modify, or delete sensitive data in a database or even gain administrative control over the application.

○ **Example**: In 2012, a major SQL injection vulnerability was exploited on the Sony Pictures website, allowing attackers to access usernames, passwords, and other sensitive data stored in the database.

3. **Cross-Site Scripting (XSS)**

○ **Description**: XSS attacks occur when attackers inject malicious scripts into websites viewed by other users. These scripts can execute in users' browsers, enabling data theft, credential capture, or unauthorized actions.

○ **Impact**: XSS vulnerabilities allow attackers to hijack sessions, steal sensitive data, or spread malware.

○ **Example**: In a popular XSS exploit, attackers injected malicious JavaScript into a forum, causing all users who visited the forum to unknowingly send their session cookies to the attacker, compromising their accounts.

4. **Cross-Site Request Forgery (CSRF)**

  o **Description**: CSRF exploits trust by tricking a user's browser into submitting unauthorized requests on another website where they are authenticated.

  o **Impact**: Attackers can perform unauthorized actions, such as changing account settings or initiating transactions, by exploiting the user's established session.

  o **Example**: If a user is logged into a banking website and unknowingly clicks on a malicious link, CSRF could trigger unauthorized fund transfers using the user's authentication session.

5. **Misconfigurations**

  o **Description**: Misconfigurations occur when systems, applications, or network devices are set up improperly, often exposing them to unnecessary risk.

  o **Impact**: Misconfigured systems can reveal sensitive information, allow unauthorized access, or create entry points for attacks.

  o **Example**: Open directories on web servers, default passwords on routers, or unnecessary services running on servers are common misconfigurations that attackers target.

6. **Unpatched Software**

   o **Description**: When software vulnerabilities are discovered, vendors release updates, or "patches," to fix these issues. Failing to apply patches leaves systems vulnerable to exploitation.

   o **Impact**: Unpatched systems are often easy targets for attackers, who can use exploits to take advantage of known vulnerabilities.

   o **Example**: The 2017 WannaCry ransomware attack spread rapidly by exploiting a known vulnerability in unpatched Windows systems, affecting hospitals, businesses, and government agencies worldwide.

7. **Weak Authentication and Authorization**

   o **Description**: Weak authentication mechanisms, such as easily guessable passwords or inadequate multi-factor authentication, make it easier for attackers to gain unauthorized access.

   o **Impact**: Attackers can exploit weak authentication to bypass login credentials, compromise accounts, and access sensitive data.

- **Example**: Credential stuffing attacks, where attackers use lists of stolen passwords to log into accounts, often succeed against systems that lack strong password policies or multi-factor authentication.

How Exploits Work

An exploit is a piece of code or software specifically designed to take advantage of a vulnerability. Exploits can vary in complexity, from simple scripts that automate known attacks to sophisticated tools that leverage multiple vulnerabilities in advanced attacks.

The Exploitation Process

1. **Reconnaissance**: Attackers begin by gathering information about the target system, identifying potential vulnerabilities. Ethical hackers perform similar reconnaissance to understand potential entry points.

2. **Identifying Vulnerabilities**: After gathering information, attackers focus on specific weaknesses, such as open ports, outdated software, or misconfigurations.

3. **Exploit Development**: Exploits are often crafted to match the vulnerability's characteristics. For instance, a buffer overflow exploit would include code designed to overflow the specific buffer in the target application.

4. **Delivery and Execution**: Exploits can be delivered through various means—email attachments, phishing links, network connections, or compromised websites. Once executed, the exploit takes advantage of the vulnerability, allowing the attacker to carry out actions like data theft, privilege escalation, or remote control.

5. **Persistence and Covering Tracks**: After gaining access, attackers may install backdoors or other mechanisms to maintain access and cover their tracks, making detection more difficult.

Example of an Exploit in Action: Buffer Overflow

In a buffer overflow exploit, an attacker identifies an application that doesn't properly check the size of incoming data. They then craft an input payload that exceeds the buffer's capacity, overwriting adjacent memory locations. If the overflow overwrites executable memory, the attacker can replace legitimate code with malicious instructions, granting control over the application and potentially the entire system.

Why Patching is Essential

Patching is the process of applying updates to software, operating systems, and applications to fix security flaws. When vendors discover vulnerabilities, they typically release patches to address these issues, protecting systems from exploitation. Failing to apply patches is one of the most common reasons systems remain vulnerable to attacks.

Benefits of Regular Patching

1. **Prevents Exploitation of Known Vulnerabilities**: As soon as vulnerabilities are publicly disclosed, attackers can quickly develop and deploy exploits to take advantage of them. Patching ensures that these weaknesses are addressed before they can be exploited.

2. **Minimizes the Attack Surface**: Each vulnerability provides a potential entry point for attackers. By patching, organizations reduce the number of exploitable weaknesses, making their systems more secure.

3. **Improves System Stability**: In addition to security, patches often fix bugs that improve software performance and reliability, helping systems run smoothly.

4. **Compliance and Regulatory Requirements**: Many industries, such as healthcare and finance, mandate regular updates to meet security standards. Failing to patch systems can lead to compliance violations and potential fines.

Challenges of Patching

Despite its importance, patching isn't always straightforward. Some challenges include:

- **Downtime**: Applying patches may require system restarts, disrupting normal operations. Organizations often schedule patching during off-hours to minimize the impact.

- **Compatibility Issues**: Some patches can cause compatibility issues with existing software or hardware. Testing patches before deployment helps ensure compatibility.

- **Patch Management**: Large organizations may have hundreds or thousands of systems, making it difficult to track and apply patches manually. Patch management software helps automate this process.

The Role of Ethical Hackers in Vulnerability and Patch Management

Ethical hackers play a critical role in vulnerability management by identifying security weaknesses before they can be exploited. By simulating attacks, ethical hackers can help organizations:

- **Identify Vulnerabilities**: Ethical hackers use tools like vulnerability scanners and manual testing to detect vulnerabilities that need to be addressed.

- **Verify Patches**: After a patch is applied, ethical hackers can test the system to confirm that the patch successfully mitigated the vulnerability and didn't introduce new issues.

- **Recommend Patch Management Solutions**: Ethical hackers advise organizations on effective patch management strategies, helping them automate and prioritize updates to stay secure.

Real-World Example of the Importance of Patching: WannaCry Ransomware Attack

The WannaCry ransomware attack in 2017 serves as a powerful example of the importance of patching. This global attack exploited a known vulnerability in Windows operating systems. Microsoft had released a patch for the vulnerability weeks before the attack, but many organizations had not yet applied it. As a result, WannaCry quickly spread across networks, encrypting files and demanding ransom payments. The attack impacted hospitals, businesses, and government institutions worldwide, demonstrating the severe consequences of delayed patching.

Understanding vulnerabilities and how exploits work is essential for ethical hackers. By identifying potential weaknesses—such as buffer overflows, SQL injections, and unpatched software—ethical hackers can help organizations prioritize security measures and minimize risk. Patching is one of the most effective ways to prevent exploitation, and ethical hackers play an important role in ensuring that vulnerabilities are properly addressed.

In the next chapter, we'll cover reconnaissance techniques, exploring methods ethical hackers use to gather information on systems and networks. Reconnaissance is a crucial step in ethical hacking, providing the information necessary for effective vulnerability assessment.

CHAPTER 8: RECONNAISSANCE TECHNIQUES (FOOT PRINTING AND SCANNING)

Reconnaissance is the first stage of ethical hacking, where hackers gather as much information as possible about a target to identify potential weaknesses. This process is essential, as it provides the foundation for planning subsequent attacks or penetration tests. Reconnaissance is typically divided into two main types—foot printing and scanning—each of which can be conducted in active or passive ways.

This chapter explores foot printing and scanning techniques, explaining the differences between active and passive methods. We'll also cover essential reconnaissance tools and exercises, including DNS lookups, whois queries, and port scanning, which help ethical hackers uncover valuable information while remaining undetected.

What is Foot printing?

Foot printing is the process of gathering information about a target's infrastructure, including IP addresses, domain names, network structures, and personnel details. The goal is to collect data that may reveal vulnerabilities or entry points without directly interacting with the target system.

There are two types of foot printing: **passive** and **active**.

1. Passive Foot printing

- **Definition**: Passive foot printing involves collecting information without directly interacting with the target system. This means using publicly available data to gather insights without alerting the target.

- **Common Techniques**:

  - o **DNS Lookups**: Checking the Domain Name System (DNS) for information about the target's domain and IP addresses.

  - o **WHOIS Queries**: Gathering information about domain ownership, registration details, and associated contact information.

  - o **Social Media and Public Records**: Using social media platforms and online records to learn about employees, systems, and locations.

Advantages of Passive Foot printing:

- It's low-risk because it doesn't directly interact with the target, reducing the chances of detection.

- It often provides high-level insights, which can be useful for social engineering or understanding the organization's structure.

2. Active Foot printing

- **Definition**: Active foot printing involves interacting directly with the target system to obtain information. This includes techniques like pinging IP addresses, scanning ports, and gathering details on live services.

- **Common Techniques**:

  o **Port Scanning**: Identifying open ports to see which services are available on a target system.

  o **Ping Sweeps**: Sending ICMP (Internet Control Message Protocol) requests to discover active hosts.

  o **Traceroute**: Mapping the path packets take to reach a network, which can reveal network structure and firewall configurations.

Advantages of Active Foot printing:

- Active techniques provide more detailed information, often necessary to identify specific vulnerabilities.

- Active foot printing reveals live systems, services, and configurations that may be critical for planning further assessments.

Ethical Considerations: Ethical hackers must have explicit authorization before performing active foot printing, as it involves direct interaction with the target system. Unauthorized active foot printing can be detected by intrusion detection systems (IDS) and is considered illegal without consent.

Hands-On Exercises: Essential Reconnaissance Techniques

To understand footprinting techniques in practice, let's explore some hands-on exercises. These exercises focus on both passive and active methods, using DNS lookups, whois queries, and port scanning.

1. DNS Lookups

DNS lookups help ethical hackers identify IP addresses associated with domain names and gain insights into a target's DNS structure, which can reveal subdomains, email servers, and more.

Tool: You can perform DNS lookups using online tools or terminal commands.

Exercise:

1. **nslookup Command** (Linux, macOS, and Windows):

     o   Open the command line and type:

bash

nslo okup example.com

o Replace example.com with the target domain. The response provides IP addresses associated with the domain, which can reveal additional servers.

2. **dig Command** (Linux and macOS):

o dig (Domain Information Groper) provides more detailed DNS information.

o Run:

bash

dig example.com

o You can also use dig to query specific DNS records:

bash

dig mx example.com

o This query returns mail exchange (MX) records, revealing the target's mail server addresses.

Interpretation: DNS lookups help identify the target's DNS structure, which can reveal email servers and subdomains that could be potential entry points.

2. WHOIS Queries

WHOIS queries provide information about domain ownership, registration dates, registrar details, and associated contact information. This information is valuable for understanding an organization's online presence and may offer leads for social engineering.

Tool: WHOIS is available as a command-line tool on Linux and macOS, and online WHOIS lookup services are widely available.

Exercise:

1. **whois Command** (Linux and macOS):

   o In the terminal, type:

bash

whois example.com

   o Replace example.com with the target domain. The response includes information about the domain registrar, registration date, expiration date, and contact information.

2. **Online WHOIS Tools**:

   o Websites like **whois.net** or **whois.domaintools.com** allow you to perform WHOIS lookups in a browser.

Interpretation: WHOIS data can reveal ownership details, allowing ethical hackers to learn more about the organization's structure. WHOIS data is also valuable for identifying domain expiration dates, which may indicate periods when security attention is reduced.

3. Port Scanning

Port scanning is a fundamental active footprinting technique used to identify open ports and available services on a target system. Each port serves a specific function, and open ports can provide clues about running services, such as web servers or databases.

Tool: Nmap (Network Mapper) is the most widely used tool for port scanning and offers various scan types.

Exercise:

1. **Basic Port Scan**:

    o   Open the terminal and run:

bash

nmap example.com

    o   Replace example.com with the target domain or IP address. This basic scan will list open ports and services.

2. **Scan Specific Ports**:

   o   To scan specific ports, use:

bash

nmap -p 80,443 example.com

   o   This command scans for HTTP (port 80) and HTTPS
       (port 443) services, which are common entry points
       for attacks.

3. **Service Version Detection**:

   o   To identify the versions of services running on open
       ports, use:

bash

nmap -sV example.com

   o   This scan reveals version details, which can help you
       identify vulnerabilities associated with specific
       software versions.

Interpretation: Port scanning helps ethical hackers map the
network, determine available services, and detect potential
vulnerabilities. For example, an outdated version of a web server
might be susceptible to known exploits.

Advanced Reconnaissance Techniques

Once basic reconnaissance is complete, ethical hackers can use advanced techniques to gather additional information.

1. Traceroute

Traceroute maps the path data packets take to reach a target, showing the routers and devices along the way. This can reveal network topology and identify firewalls or load balancers.

Exercise:

1. **Run Traceroute** (Linux/macOS):

bash

traceroute example.com

   o On Windows, use tracert instead of traceroute.

2. **Interpretation**: Traceroute results show each hop (device or router) along the path to the target. This helps ethical hackers understand network paths and potential chokepoints that could be targeted or monitored.

2. Banner Grabbing

Banner grabbing involves capturing messages or "banners" that some services display when connected, which often include information about the software version and operating system.

Exercise:

1. **Using Netcat (nc)**:

    o Connect to a specific port to capture the banner:

bash

nc example.com 80

    o Type HEAD / HTTP/1.1 followed by pressing Enter twice to get the HTTP server's banner.

Interpretation: Banners provide insights into software versions and OS types, which can be useful for vulnerability identification. Outdated or misconfigured software often reveals detailed information in banners, giving attackers clues about potential exploits.

Using Reconnaissance to Inform Further Testing

Reconnaissance results provide valuable information for planning the next stages of ethical hacking. Based on the data collected, ethical hackers can:

- **Identify high-risk services**: For example, open ports running outdated versions of FTP, SSH, or HTTP might require further testing.

- **Map the network**: Understanding the network's structure and connected devices helps ethical hackers simulate realistic attack paths.

- **Prioritize vulnerabilities**: Certain findings, such as visible email servers or unsecured FTP ports, are prioritized in penetration testing for further examination.

Note: All active reconnaissance, such as port scanning, should only be performed with explicit permission from the target organization to avoid unauthorized access violations.

Reconnaissance is a critical phase of ethical hacking, providing essential information that helps shape the strategy for testing and securing a target system. Passive footprinting allows ethical hackers to gather information discreetly, while active footprinting, such as port scanning and traceroute, reveals more detailed data for identifying vulnerabilities.

In the next chapter, we'll delve into social engineering techniques, exploring how attackers can exploit human vulnerabilities to gain unauthorized access. Social engineering requires skill and understanding of psychology, making it a powerful tool that complements technical reconnaissance methods.

CHAPTER 9: SOCIAL ENGINEERING AND HUMAN VULNERABILITIES

While technical vulnerabilities are often the focus of cybersecurity, human vulnerabilities are equally critical and often more easily exploited. Social engineering is the art of manipulating individuals into divulging confidential information, granting access, or performing actions that compromise security. Ethical hackers need a thorough understanding of social engineering tactics to help organizations protect against these human-centered attacks.

In this chapter, we'll examine common social engineering techniques, discuss why they're so effective, and provide real-world examples. You'll also find exercises that simulate social engineering in ethical, controlled environments.

What is Social Engineering?

Social engineering is a manipulation technique that exploits human psychology rather than relying solely on technical methods. It's one of the oldest and most effective ways to compromise systems, as it targets people's trust, curiosity, and sense of urgency. Common goals of social engineering include gaining unauthorized access, obtaining sensitive information, and spreading malware.

Why Social Engineering is Effective

Social engineering is highly effective for several reasons:

- **Trust**: People are generally inclined to trust others, especially if they appear legitimate or in authority.

- **Fear and Urgency**: Attackers create a sense of urgency or fear to compel individuals to act without fully assessing the situation (e.g., "You must reset your password immediately to prevent account suspension!").

- **Lack of Awareness**: Many people are unaware of social engineering tactics, making them vulnerable to deception.

- **Information Overload**: With the constant influx of emails, messages, and tasks, individuals may let their guard down and fail to verify requests.

Common Social Engineering Tactics

1. **Phishing**

   o **Description**: Phishing is a tactic where attackers impersonate legitimate entities to deceive individuals into revealing sensitive information, such as usernames, passwords, or financial data.

   o **Method**: Phishing attacks are typically delivered via email, with messages that look like official correspondence from banks, online services, or colleagues.

- o **Example**: An email that appears to be from a bank asks the user to click a link and enter their account details to "verify" their account.

2. **Spear Phishing**

   - o **Description**: Spear phishing is a more targeted form of phishing aimed at specific individuals or organizations, often using personal information to increase credibility.

   - o **Method**: Attackers research the target's role, contacts, or company details to tailor their message.

   - o **Example**: A CFO receives an email appearing to be from the CEO, asking them to authorize a large transfer for a "confidential" acquisition.

3. **Pretexting**

   - o **Description**: Pretexting involves creating a fabricated scenario, or pretext, to persuade the target to provide sensitive information or access.

   - o **Method**: Attackers often pretend to be someone in authority, such as an IT support technician, or a colleague needing immediate assistance.

- o **Example**: An attacker calls an employee, claiming to be from IT and asking for their login credentials to fix a "technical issue."

4. **Baiting**

- o **Description**: Baiting relies on enticing targets with something attractive, like free software, to trick them into downloading malware or entering personal information.

- o **Method**: Baiting often takes the form of free music, movies, or software downloads. Sometimes, attackers use USB drives left in public places, hoping someone will plug it in.

- o **Example**: A USB drive labeled "Confidential: Employee Salaries" is left in a break room. When someone plugs it into a computer, malware is installed.

5. **Tailgating (or Piggybacking)**

- o **Description**: Tailgating is a physical social engineering tactic where an unauthorized person gains access to a secure area by following an authorized individual.

- o **Method**: Attackers might pretend to have forgotten their access card or simply walk closely behind someone entering a secure area.

- o **Example**: An attacker follows an employee into a restricted area, claiming they "left their badge at home."

6. **Quid Pro Quo**

- o **Description**: Quid pro quo attacks involve offering something in exchange for information or access, exploiting people's natural tendency to reciprocate.

- o **Method**: Attackers might pose as IT support and offer to "help" solve a technical issue in exchange for login credentials.

- o **Example**: A caller claims to be from a technical support team, offering free help with a computer issue if the target provides their login details.

Real-World Examples of Social Engineering Attacks

1. **The Twitter Hack (2020)**

- o **What Happened**: Attackers conducted a social engineering attack on Twitter employees, tricking them into revealing credentials to internal tools.

Once inside, attackers took over several high-profile accounts to promote a cryptocurrency scam.

o **Impact**: The attack affected well-known accounts (e.g., Elon Musk, Barack Obama) and resulted in millions of followers seeing the scam message, damaging Twitter's reputation.

o **Lesson**: Employee training on social engineering tactics, particularly phishing and pretexting, is essential to prevent unauthorized access.

2. **The RSA Security Breach (2011)**

o **What Happened**: Attackers used a phishing email targeting RSA employee with a subject line "2011 Recruitment Plan." The email contained a malicious Excel attachment. Once opened, the malware exploited a vulnerability and allowed attackers to steal data, including valuable cryptographic keys.

o **Impact**: The breach compromised RSA's security token systems, which many organizations used to secure their own networks.

o **Lesson**: Even trusted security companies are vulnerable to social engineering. Clear email filtering and employee awareness can reduce the risk.

Hands-On Exercises: Practicing Social Engineering Safely

While ethical hackers avoid real-world social engineering without explicit consent, there are ethical, controlled ways to practice these techniques in simulated environments. Here are some exercises to help you develop social engineering awareness and skills.

1. Creating a Phishing Simulation

Phishing simulations help ethical hackers understand how phishing attacks are constructed and identify signs of phishing emails.

Exercise:

- **Step 1**: Create a mock phishing email. Use a free email account and send a message to yourself or a test account, pretending to be a known service (e.g., a bank or online store).

- **Step 2**: Include common phishing elements, like urgent language ("Your account will be suspended!"), a link to a mock login page, and logos that mimic real branding.

- **Step 3**: Review the email and take note of phishing indicators, such as the sender's address, spelling errors, and mismatched URLs. This exercise improves your ability to spot real phishing emails.

Note: Never conduct this exercise on live email accounts without explicit consent. Phishing simulations should be limited to personal or testing environments.

2. Role-Playing Pretexting Scenarios

Pretexting exercises help you practice creating believable scenarios without malicious intent. In this exercise, you'll role-play different pretexting scenarios in a controlled setting.

Exercise:

- **Step 1**: Choose a scenario, such as an IT support representative requesting information from an employee.

- **Step 2**: Develop a script for the pretext, including questions you might ask, such as "I'm verifying your account, could you confirm your username?"

- **Step 3**: Role-play with a colleague or friend (with their consent), practicing responses and refining your approach to seem credible.

Goal: The goal is to recognize how pretexting works and to become familiar with the red flags of pretexting attempts.

3. Investigating a Quid Pro Quo Scenario

This exercise simulates how attackers use quid pro quo to gain trust. By practicing scenarios like these, you'll be better prepared to recognize and resist similar real-world tactics.

Exercise:

- **Step 1**: Prepare a scenario where you're offering "technical support" for a specific problem (e.g., "free" password recovery assistance).

- **Step 2**: Role-play the scenario, asking the target to provide information for "assistance," such as login details.

- **Step 3**: After the role-play, discuss with your partner the potential signs they noticed that might indicate a social engineering attempt.

Note: This exercise helps illustrate how attackers use reciprocity to gain trust and serves as a valuable learning tool for ethical hackers to recognize quid pro quo attacks.

Preventing Social Engineering Attacks

Social engineering is challenging to defend against, but there are effective ways to reduce risk:

1. **Security Awareness Training**: Regular training sessions help employees recognize phishing emails, suspicious requests, and the signs of social engineering attempts.

2. **Multi-Factor Authentication (MFA)**: MFA requires users to confirm their identity in multiple ways, reducing the risk of attackers gaining access through stolen credentials.

3. **Email Filtering and Security Software**: Advanced email filters and security software can block common phishing emails and flag suspicious links.

4. **Verification Protocols**: Organizations should establish verification processes, requiring employees to verify the identity of anyone requesting sensitive information.

5. **Physical Security Measures**: Tailgating and unauthorized access can be prevented by installing secure access controls, like keycards and biometric scanners, and by educating employees to challenge unknown individuals in secure areas.

Social engineering targets human vulnerabilities, using psychological manipulation rather than technical exploits. By understanding tactics like phishing, pretexting, and quid pro quo, ethical hackers can help organizations implement defenses to counter these techniques. This chapter's exercises provide hands-on ways to explore social engineering tactics in controlled environments, enabling ethical hackers to build awareness without causing harm.

In the next chapter, we'll examine initial access techniques used to infiltrate systems and networks. Understanding how attackers gain access is crucial for ethical hackers, as it provides insights into preventing unauthorized entry and strengthening defenses.

CHAPTER 10: GAINING INITIAL ACCESS (BREAKING INTO SYSTEMS)

In the context of ethical hacking and penetration testing, gaining initial access refers to the process of finding and exploiting entry points to break into a target system or network. The goal is to simulate real-world attacks to identify potential security gaps before malicious actors can exploit them. Gaining initial access is a critical phase in penetration testing, as it reveals vulnerabilities that could allow unauthorized access to sensitive data and systems.

This chapter introduces tools and techniques commonly used to gain initial access in authorized penetration tests, including brute-force attacks, phishing simulations, and the ethical considerations surrounding these methods.

The Role of Initial Access in Penetration Testing

Initial access is the gateway to deeper system penetration. Ethical hackers seek to identify and exploit vulnerabilities that allow access to systems, which can reveal weak points in user authentication, network security, or application defenses. Gaining access to a system can involve:

- Exploiting weak passwords or unpatched vulnerabilities.

- Phishing to trick users into revealing credentials.

- Targeting open ports and services that could be entry points.

Because initial access techniques often mimic those of malicious actors, ethical hackers must have explicit authorization from the organization being tested. Ethical hacking relies on a clear scope of engagement and agreed-upon techniques, ensuring that all testing is conducted legally and responsibly.

Common Techniques for Gaining Initial Access

1. Brute-Force Attacks

A brute-force attack is a method in which an attacker systematically tries all possible combinations of passwords or encryption keys to gain access to a system. While time-consuming, brute-force attacks can be successful against weak passwords or where rate-limiting isn't enforced.

- **Types of Brute-Force Attacks**:
    - **Simple Brute-Force**: Attempts all possible character combinations until the correct password is found.

    - **Dictionary Attack**: Uses a predefined list of commonly used passwords or words (a "dictionary") to guess the password.

    - **Hybrid Attack**: Combines dictionary attacks with brute-force techniques, appending numbers or special characters to each word in the dictionary.

- **Tools for Brute-Forcing**:

    o **Hydra**: A powerful tool that performs fast brute-force attacks on various protocols (HTTP, FTP, SSH, etc.).

    o **John the Ripper**: Often used for password cracking, especially for testing weak passwords in Unix systems.

    o **Medusa**: Similar to Hydra, Medusa supports a range of protocols and is designed for fast brute-forcing.

Exercise: Ethical Brute-Forcing with Hydra:

1. **Setup**: Use a test environment with a known target (e.g., a local HTTP server with a test login page).

2. **Command**:

bash

Copy code

hydra -l admin -P /path/to/password/list.txt http-post-form "login.php:username=^USER^&password=^PASS^:Invalid login"

    o **Explanation**: Hydra tries each password in the list against the "admin" username. If successful, it will reveal the correct password.

Ethical Considerations: Brute-force attacks generate significant traffic and are easily detectable, so ethical hackers should use them only on test systems or with explicit authorization. Real-world applications should implement strong password policies and rate-limiting to counter brute-force attempts.

2. Phishing Attacks

Phishing is a technique where attackers craft emails, websites, or messages that impersonate trusted entities to trick users into revealing credentials or downloading malware. Phishing is highly effective because it exploits human trust and curiosity.

- **Types of Phishing**:

    - **Email Phishing**: Sending emails that appear to be from trusted sources, such as a bank or colleague, to convince users to click on a malicious link or provide login credentials.

    - **Spear Phishing**: A targeted form of phishing that customizes messages for a specific individual or group, often using personal information to increase credibility.

    - **Clone Phishing**: Creating a nearly identical copy of a legitimate email but altering a link or attachment to include malware.

- **Phishing Tools**:

    o **Gophish**: An open-source phishing framework that allows penetration testers to create, send, and analyze phishing campaigns.

    o **Social-Engineer Toolkit (SET)**: SET includes a phishing module that can create fake login pages or launch email phishing attacks for testing purposes.

Exercise: Ethical Phishing Simulation with Gophish:

1. **Setup**: Configure Gophish on a test server to send a simulated phishing email.

2. **Create a Campaign**:

    o Design an email template that resembles a common company notification, such as a password reset request.

3. **Launch the Campaign**:

    o Send the phishing email to test accounts within the controlled environment.

4. **Analyze Results**:

    o Track responses and identify how many recipients clicked on the link, entered credentials, or reported the email as phishing.

Ethical Considerations: Ethical phishing simulations require strict guidelines and are often limited to testing environments or consenting participants. Organizations should notify users about ongoing awareness programs, and ethical hackers must respect privacy and confidentiality when analyzing results.

3. Exploiting Vulnerabilities and Weak Configurations

Exploiting vulnerabilities in software or configurations is another common way to gain initial access. These vulnerabilities can range from unpatched software to insecure settings, such as open ports or unnecessary services.

- **Types of Vulnerability Exploits**:

    - **Unpatched Software**: Many attacks exploit known vulnerabilities in unpatched software versions, such as outdated web servers or databases.

    - **Weak Default Configurations**: Many systems ship with default credentials or configurations that are left unchanged, making them easy targets.

    - **Exposed Services and Ports**: Open ports, such as SSH (22), FTP (21), or RDP (3389), can provide entry points for attackers if they are not adequately secured.

- **Tools for Vulnerability Exploitation**:

- o **Metasploit Framework**: A powerful tool that includes a range of exploits for different vulnerabilities, enabling ethical hackers to simulate real-world attacks.

- o **Nessus**: A vulnerability scanner that identifies weaknesses in systems, such as outdated software or weak configurations.

Exercise: Using Metasploit to Exploit a Vulnerability:

1. **Setup**: Use Metasploit with a known test vulnerability, such as the outdated "vsftpd" FTP server with a backdoor.

2. **Command**:

bash

msfconsole

use exploit/unix/ftp/vsftpd_234_backdoor

set RHOST [target IP]

exploit

- o **Explanation**: This command uses Metasploit to target an unpatched vsftpd vulnerability, demonstrating how attackers might gain access through known exploits.

Ethical Considerations: Vulnerability exploitation should only be conducted on systems where the ethical hacker has explicit permission, and all tests should follow documented procedures to prevent unintended harm to the system.

Protecting Against Initial Access Techniques

Ethical hackers can recommend security measures that protect systems from initial access attacks:

1. **Implement Strong Password Policies**:

   o Enforce minimum complexity requirements for passwords, encourage the use of passphrases, and regularly rotate passwords to protect against brute-force attacks.

2. **Enable Multi-Factor Authentication (MFA)**:

   o MFA adds an extra layer of security beyond passwords, requiring users to verify their identity through multiple means, like a code on a mobile device.

3. **User Awareness and Phishing Training**:

   o Regular training helps users identify and report phishing attempts. Awareness programs can greatly reduce the success of phishing attacks.

4. **Apply Regular Patching and Software Updates**:

   o   Keeping software up to date and applying patches as soon as they're released helps reduce the risk of exploitation from known vulnerabilities.

5. **Disable Unnecessary Services and Close Unused Ports**:

   o   By limiting the number of open ports and disabling services that aren't needed, organizations reduce their attack surface and make it harder for attackers to gain access.

6. **Enforce Account Lockout Policies**:

   o   Implementing lockout policies after a certain number of failed login attempts helps mitigate the risk of brute-force attacks.

Ethical and Legal Considerations in Initial Access Testing

Because initial access testing closely resembles real-world attacks, ethical hackers must follow strict ethical and legal guidelines:

- **Scope and Authorization**: Ensure that all tests are within the agreed scope and that written permission has been granted for every system or network being tested.

- **Controlled Environments for Phishing**: Phishing simulations should be limited to test groups with informed consent to avoid privacy breaches.

- **Data Confidentiality**: Respect confidentiality and avoid collecting more data than necessary during tests. Store any data obtained securely and ensure it's deleted once testing is complete.

Ethical hackers should clearly document each step and report findings responsibly, ensuring transparency and accountability throughout the testing process.

Gaining initial access is a critical stage of penetration testing, enabling ethical hackers to identify weaknesses that could be exploited by attackers. Techniques like brute-force attacks, phishing, and vulnerability exploitation simulate real-world entry points, helping organizations understand and mitigate potential threats.

In the next chapter, we'll explore privilege escalation techniques, discussing how attackers can elevate their permissions once inside a system. Understanding privilege escalation is key to securing sensitive data and preventing unauthorized access within an organization's network.

CHAPTER 11: EXPLOITATION AND PRIVILEGE ESCALATION

Once an ethical hacker gains initial access to a system, the next step often involves exploiting additional vulnerabilities to elevate privileges, gaining access to restricted resources or administrative controls. Privilege escalation is a critical phase in penetration testing, as it demonstrates how attackers might increase their access and control within a system. This chapter covers the basics of privilege escalation, methods for identifying exploitable vulnerabilities, and hands-on exercises for common privilege escalation techniques.

What is Privilege Escalation?

Privilege escalation occurs when an attacker with limited access to a system finds a way to increase their permissions, potentially gaining administrative or root-level control. Privilege escalation can be classified into two main types:

1. **Vertical Privilege Escalation**: When a user with low privileges (e.g., a standard user) gains higher privileges, such as those of an administrator or root user.

2. **Horizontal Privilege Escalation**: When a user gains access to another user's permissions or resources without necessarily increasing their overall privilege level (e.g., a user accessing another user's files).

Privilege escalation exploits often rely on:

- **Weak System Configurations**: Misconfigured permissions, unpatched software, and default settings.

- **Known Vulnerabilities**: Exploits that target specific software flaws or outdated components.

- **Insecure Processes and Services**: Services running with unnecessary privileges or applications that fail to properly validate user permissions.

Understanding privilege escalation methods helps ethical hackers test and recommend ways to secure sensitive resources, ensuring that attackers cannot compromise critical system components.

Common Privilege Escalation Techniques

1. **Exploiting Misconfigured File and Folder Permissions**

Files and folders with misconfigured permissions can be used to elevate privileges. For example, if system files or executables are writable by standard users, an attacker could modify them to run malicious code with elevated privileges.

   o **Example**: A configuration file that stores sensitive information (such as passwords or database credentials) is readable by all users, allowing an attacker to access this information.

o **Tool**: ls -l in Linux or icacls in Windows can help ethical hackers view permissions on files and directories.

2. Abusing SUID/GUID Binaries in Linux

In Linux, certain binaries are set with special permissions called **Set User ID (SUID)** or **Set Group ID (GUID)**, which allow them to execute with elevated privileges, typically root. If these binaries are misconfigured or vulnerable, attackers can exploit them to gain root privileges.

o **Example**: If an SUID binary allows standard users to execute commands with root privileges, modifying this binary or injecting commands can grant root access.

o **Tool**: The find command can be used to locate SUID/GUID binaries:

bash

find / -perm -u=s -type f 2>/dev/null

3. Exploiting Unpatched Software and Kernel Vulnerabilities

Software vulnerabilities, especially in the kernel, can be exploited to escalate privileges. Kernel exploits are particularly dangerous because they provide attackers with control over the entire system.

- o **Example**: Exploiting a known kernel vulnerability in an outdated Linux or Windows version can allow attackers to bypass user restrictions and gain root or administrator access.

- o **Tool**: Metasploit provides a variety of privilege escalation exploits, which can be tested against known vulnerabilities in target systems.

4. **DLL Hijacking in Windows**

In Windows, **Dynamic Link Libraries (DLLs)** are files that provide functions and resources for executable files. DLL hijacking occurs when an application is tricked into loading a malicious DLL instead of the legitimate one, potentially granting an attacker higher privileges if the application runs with elevated permissions.

- o **Example**: An attacker places a malicious DLL in the application directory with the same name as a legitimate DLL, causing the application to load the malicious one.

- o **Tool**: Tools like Process Monitor can help identify DLLs being loaded by applications, which ethical hackers can use to locate potential DLL hijacking opportunities.

5. **Exploiting Weak Service Configurations in Windows**

Services in Windows often run with system-level privileges. If a service is misconfigured—such as having insecure file paths or weak permissions—an attacker can manipulate it to execute code with elevated privileges.

- o **Example**: If a service is set to run automatically with a non-secure path (e.g., C:\Program Files\My Service\service.exe), an attacker could replace service.exe with malicious code.

- o **Tool**: Windows services can be viewed and modified using the sc command, and tools like AccessChk can check permissions on service files.

Hands-On Exercises: Common Privilege Escalation Methods

These exercises will help you practice privilege escalation techniques in controlled, ethical environments.

Exercise 1: Linux SUID Binary Exploitation

Objective: Practice privilege escalation by identifying and exploiting an SUID binary.

1. **Setup**: Create a test SUID binary on a Linux system (if one is available with authorized access).

2. **Command**: Use find to search for binaries with SUID permissions.

bash

find / -perm -u=s -type f 2>/dev/null

3. **Exploit**: If a vulnerable SUID binary is found, execute it to check if it runs with elevated permissions. In a controlled lab, you might create a file owned by root with SUID enabled, running a command with root privileges.

Note: SUID exploitation can potentially compromise the system, so this should be conducted in a secure test environment only.

Exercise 2: Windows DLL Hijacking Simulation

Objective: Use DLL hijacking to simulate privilege escalation in a Windows environment.

1. **Setup**: Identify a program or service that loads DLLs with elevated permissions.

2. **Monitor DLL Loading**:

   o Use Process Monitor to identify DLLs loaded by the target application.

3. **Replace DLL**: Create a DLL with the same name as the original but containing a harmless payload, then place it in the application's directory.

4. **Execution**: Run the application to verify if the malicious DLL is loaded instead of the legitimate one.

ETHICAL HACKING: A HANDS-ON GUIDE FOR BEGINNERS

Note: Be cautious and avoid deploying harmful payloads. Practice in isolated environments with permission.

Exercise 3: Abusing Weak Service Permissions in Windows

Objective: Simulate privilege escalation by exploiting a weakly configured Windows service.

1. **Setup**: Identify a service running with SYSTEM privileges and check if the service binary path is writable.

   o Use sc qc <service-name> to display service configuration.

   o Use AccessChk from Sysinternals to confirm if you have write access to the service path.

2. **Replace Service Binary**:

   o Replace the binary with a file or executable of your choice that could escalate privileges when the service restarts.

3. **Restart the Service**:

   o Restart the service with net start <service-name> and verify if the modified executable runs with elevated privileges.

Note: This exercise should only be performed in a testing environment with appropriate permissions, as modifying services on live systems can disrupt operations.

Mitigating Privilege Escalation Risks

To help organizations defend against privilege escalation, ethical hackers can recommend these preventive measures:

1. **Apply Least Privilege Principle**:

   o Limit user and service permissions to only what is necessary. Avoid granting administrator or root access unless essential.

2. **Keep Software and Systems Updated**:

   o Regular updates and patches reduce the risk of known vulnerabilities that attackers can exploit.

3. **Secure SUID/GUID Binaries and Services**:

   o Remove or restrict SUID/GUID binaries on Linux, and configure Windows services to use secure paths and permissions.

4. **Implement Access Controls and Audits**:

   o Regularly audit permissions and access logs, ensuring that sensitive files and services are not accessible by non-privileged users.

5. **Monitor for Exploit Indicators**:

   o   Monitor for unusual activity, such as changes in SUID binaries, suspicious DLL loads, or attempts to restart services, which may indicate privilege escalation attempts.

Ethical and Legal Considerations in Privilege Escalation Testing

Privilege escalation exercises often require elevated permissions and direct interaction with system configurations. Therefore, ethical hackers should:

- **Define Clear Boundaries**: Ensure that the scope of testing is clear, specifying which systems, files, and services can be modified or tested for privilege escalation.

- **Limit Tests to Authorized Environments**: Privilege escalation tests should be performed only in isolated test environments or with explicit permission on production systems.

- **Report Vulnerabilities with Solutions**: When vulnerabilities are identified, provide a detailed report with recommendations for mitigating privilege escalation risks.

Documenting all actions, obtaining explicit authorization, and prioritizing transparency are essential to maintain ethical standards in privilege escalation testing.

Privilege escalation is a critical aspect of penetration testing, demonstrating how attackers might exploit system vulnerabilities to increase access and control. Through techniques like SUID exploitation, DLL hijacking, and exploiting weak service configurations, ethical hackers can help organizations identify risks and secure their systems.

In the next chapter, we'll explore wireless network hacking, discussing the vulnerabilities in Wi-Fi networks, tools for wireless assessment, and methods for ethically testing wireless security. Understanding wireless vulnerabilities is crucial in today's mobile and IoT-driven environments, where networks are often extended to public spaces.

CHAPTER 12: WIRELESS NETWORK HACKING

Wireless networks are widely used in homes, businesses, and public spaces, offering convenient internet access for multiple devices. However, their reliance on radio signals makes them more vulnerable to unauthorized access and attacks compared to wired networks. Wireless network hacking focuses on identifying and exploiting these weaknesses to understand potential threats and improve security.

In this chapter, we'll discuss Wi-Fi security standards, common vulnerabilities, and ethical techniques for Wi-Fi auditing. This knowledge helps ethical hackers identify weak points in wireless networks and recommend best practices to enhance security.

Wi-Fi Security Standards and Their Weaknesses

Wi-Fi security protocols protect data and control access on wireless networks. Over the years, several standards have been developed, each with its strengths and weaknesses. Let's review the main Wi-Fi security standards:

1. WEP (Wired Equivalent Privacy)

- **Description**: WEP was the first Wi-Fi security protocol, introduced in 1997. It uses a static encryption key to protect data, aiming to make wireless networks as secure as wired ones.

- **Weaknesses**:

  o **Weak Encryption**: WEP's 40-bit encryption key can be cracked quickly with readily available tools.

  o **Reused IVs (Initialization Vectors)**: WEP reuses IVs, making it easier for attackers to decipher the encryption key.

- **Current Status**: WEP is now considered obsolete and insecure. Most devices and routers no longer support WEP due to its vulnerabilities.

2. WPA (Wi-Fi Protected Access)

- **Description**: WPA was introduced as an interim improvement over WEP, with stronger encryption methods and dynamic keys. It uses TKIP (Temporal Key Integrity Protocol) for encryption, which dynamically changes the encryption key for each data packet.

- **Weaknesses**:

  o **Susceptible to TKIP Attacks**: TKIP is more secure than WEP but still has vulnerabilities that make WPA insecure.

  o **Backward Compatibility**: WPA maintained compatibility with older devices, which limited its security enhancements.

- **Current Status**: WPA is an improvement over WEP but still considered weak by modern standards. WPA2 has since replaced it.

3. WPA2 (Wi-Fi Protected Access 2)

- **Description**: WPA2 is the most widely used Wi-Fi security protocol today, using AES (Advanced Encryption Standard) for encryption. WPA2-PSK (Pre-Shared Key) is used for personal networks, while WPA2-Enterprise is preferred in corporate environments.

- **Weaknesses**:

    o **KRACK Attack**: The Key Reinstallation Attack (KRACK) exploits a flaw in WPA2's four-way handshake process, allowing attackers to decrypt or inject packets.

    o **Weak Password Vulnerability**: WPA2-PSK is vulnerable to brute-force attacks if weak passwords are used.

- **Current Status**: WPA2 remains secure if configured properly, but WPA3 is gradually replacing it due to its enhanced security.

4. WPA3

- **Description**: WPA3 is the latest Wi-Fi security standard, addressing weaknesses in WPA2 by offering improved encryption, mutual authentication, and protection against brute-force attacks. WPA3 uses SAE (Simultaneous Authentication of Equals) instead of the pre-shared key approach, making it more resilient.

- **Weaknesses**:

    o **Device Compatibility**: Older devices may not support WPA3, limiting its widespread adoption.

    o **Dragonblood Vulnerability**: Researchers found a vulnerability in WPA3's SAE handshake (the Dragonblood attack), which can be mitigated through updates.

- **Current Status**: WPA3 is currently the most secure Wi-Fi standard available and is recommended for new networks.

Summary: For optimal security, networks should avoid WEP and WPA, opting instead for WPA2 or WPA3. WPA3 provides the strongest security, but WPA2 with a strong password and regular updates remains a solid choice for many networks.

Common Wireless Attacks

1. **Rogue Access Points**: Attackers set up unauthorized access points near a target network, mimicking the legitimate network's SSID (network name). Users unknowingly connect to the rogue access point, allowing attackers to intercept data.

2. **Evil Twin Attack**: Similar to a rogue access point, the attacker creates an access point with the same SSID as a legitimate network. Users connect to it, and attackers intercept sensitive data or redirect users to malicious sites.

3. **Deauthentication Attack**: In this attack, attackers send deauthentication packets to disconnect users from a Wi-Fi network. Once disconnected, users may be tricked into connecting to a rogue access point.

4. **WPA2 Handshake Capture and Dictionary Attack**: Attackers capture the WPA2 handshake between a client and the access point during connection. Then, they attempt to crack the password by brute-forcing or using a dictionary attack.

5. **KRACK Attack (Key Reinstallation Attack)**: KRACK exploits a vulnerability in the WPA2 protocol, allowing attackers to decrypt, replay, or inject packets. While the attack can't capture the initial handshake, it allows attackers to eavesdrop on previously secure communications.

6. **Wi-Fi Protected Setup (WPS) PIN Attack**: WPS is a feature intended to simplify network setup, but it's vulnerable to brute-force attacks. An attacker can crack the PIN and gain access to the network, even if WPA2 is used.

Real-World Applications: Ethical Wi-Fi Auditing Techniques

Ethical hackers use a variety of tools and methods to audit Wi-Fi networks, ensuring they are secure against common attacks. Here are some ethical Wi-Fi auditing techniques:

1. Network Discovery and Packet Analysis

Network discovery tools help ethical hackers identify available Wi-Fi networks and understand their configurations. Packet analysis tools, meanwhile, capture and analyze data packets, offering insights into network vulnerabilities.

- **Tool: Airodump-ng**

    o **Usage**: Airodump-ng, part of the Aircrack-ng suite, is a tool that captures packets and displays information about wireless networks, including SSIDs, signal strength, encryption types, and connected clients.

    o **Exercise**:

        1. Open a terminal and run Airodump-ng:

bash

sudo airodump-ng wlan0

- Replace wlan0 with your wireless network adapter's name.

2. Observe the networks available and note details like encryption types and channel numbers.

- **Tool: Wireshark**

    o **Usage**: Wireshark is a packet analyzer that captures and inspects data packets. It's useful for identifying unusual traffic or protocol vulnerabilities.

    o **Exercise**:

    1. Start Wireshark and set the network interface to monitor mode.

    2. Capture packets and analyze data to identify unencrypted or insecure communications.

    3. Look for packets showing open network protocols or suspect traffic patterns.

2. WPA/WPA2 Handshake Capture and Password Cracking

In WPA2 networks, ethical hackers can capture the handshake and attempt to crack the password using brute-force or dictionary attacks.

- **Tool**: **Airodump-ng and Aircrack-ng**

  - **Usage**: Airodump-ng captures the WPA handshake, while Aircrack-ng attempts to crack the captured handshake using a dictionary of passwords.

  - **Exercise**:

    1. Capture the WPA handshake with Airodump-ng:

bash

sudo airodump-ng -c [channel] --bssid [BSSID] -w [filename] wlan0

- Replace [channel] with the channel number, [BSSID] with the target's BSSID, and [filename] with the output file name.

    2. Use Aircrack-ng to crack the password:

bash

aircrack-ng -w /path/to/password/list.txt -b [BSSID] [filename].cap

    3. Analyze results and note any successful cracks.

Ethical Considerations: Always conduct WPA handshake capture and cracking tests on networks where you have explicit permission. Unauthorized Wi-Fi cracking is illegal.

3. Rogue Access Point Detection

Rogue access points are unauthorized Wi-Fi networks that mimic legitimate ones. Ethical hackers can detect and remove rogue access points to protect users from connecting to malicious networks.

- **Tool**: **Kismet**

  - o **Usage**: Kismet is a wireless network detector that identifies and logs Wi-Fi networks, distinguishing legitimate access points from potential rogue APs.

  - o **Exercise**:

    1. Run Kismet in monitor mode on a network adapter to identify rogue access points.

    2. Analyze Kismet's output to see SSIDs and compare them with known, legitimate networks.

    3. Use Kismet to locate rogue access points by signal strength.

Best Practice: Organizations should regularly scan for rogue access points to prevent unauthorized network access.

4. Testing WPS Vulnerability

WPS PIN attacks target networks with Wi-Fi Protected Setup enabled, as the WPS PIN can be brute-forced to gain access.

- **Tool**: **Reaver**

  - **Usage**: Reaver is a tool for testing WPS PIN vulnerabilities, attempting to brute-force the PIN to gain network access.

  - **Exercise**:

    1. Run Reaver to test WPS on a vulnerable network:

bash

sudo reaver -i wlan0 -b [BSSID] -c [channel] -vv

      - Replace [BSSID] and [channel] with the target network's details.

    2. Monitor Reaver's progress as it tries different PIN combinations to access the network.

Ethical Considerations: WPS testing should only be performed on authorized networks. Disable WPS on routers whenever possible to improve security.

Best Practices for Securing Wireless Networks

After testing wireless security, ethical hackers can recommend these practices to organizations:

1. **Use WPA3 or WPA2 with Strong Passwords**: Avoid WEP and WPA. Use WPA3 whenever possible, and if using WPA2, ensure passwords are long and complex.

2. **Disable WPS**: WPS is convenient but highly vulnerable to brute-force attacks. Disabling WPS adds an extra layer of security.

3. **Regularly Update Firmware**: Update router firmware to protect against known vulnerabilities and ensure the latest security features are active.

4. **Set Up a Guest Network**: Use a separate network for guests to protect internal resources and sensitive data.

5. **Monitor for Rogue Access Points**: Regularly scan the environment to detect and remove unauthorized access points.

6. **Enable Network Segmentation**: Isolate critical systems from public or less secure networks to limit exposure in case of a breach.

Ethical and Legal Considerations in Wireless Hacking

Wireless network testing closely simulates real-world attacks, so ethical hackers must:

- **Obtain Explicit Authorization**: Only test networks where you have documented permission, as unauthorized Wi-Fi hacking is illegal.

- **Use Non-Destructive Techniques**: Avoid attacks like deauthentication on production networks, as they can disrupt legitimate users.

- **Respect Privacy**: When analyzing packets or data, avoid collecting personal information and follow organizational data privacy guidelines.

Document all findings and provide actionable security recommendations to improve the organization's wireless security.

Wireless network hacking allows ethical hackers to identify weaknesses in Wi-Fi networks and ensure secure configurations. By understanding wireless standards, common vulnerabilities, and ethical Wi-Fi auditing techniques, ethical hackers can help organizations protect their networks from unauthorized access.

In the next chapter, we'll cover web application hacking, discussing how ethical hackers assess web applications for vulnerabilities like SQL injection, cross-site scripting, and more. Web application security is increasingly critical as organizations rely on web-based services for their operations.

Chapter 13: Web Application Hacking

As the internet has evolved, web applications have become integral to how businesses operate, providing everything from e-commerce to banking, social networking, and more. However, the popularity and complexity of web applications also make them prime targets for attackers. Web application hacking involves testing and securing web-based applications to protect against common vulnerabilities that can compromise data and system integrity.

In this chapter, we'll cover the basics of how web applications function, explore common vulnerabilities like Cross-Site Scripting (XSS) and Cross-Site Request Forgery (CSRF), and provide example scenarios that help ethical hackers practice securing web applications.

How Websites and Web Applications Work

Web applications operate on a client-server model, where users (clients) access services hosted on a web server. Here's a quick overview of how they work:

1. **Client Side**: The client side, also known as the frontend, is the part of a web application that users interact with in their browsers. It typically includes HTML, CSS, and JavaScript, which handle the layout, styling, and interactivity of web pages.

2. **Server Side**: The server side, or backend, includes the web server and database. The server processes requests from clients, retrieves or manipulates data, and sends responses back to the client.

3. **HTTP and HTTPS Protocols**: Web applications communicate via HTTP or HTTPS protocols. HTTP is unencrypted, while HTTPS encrypts data for secure transmission, making HTTPS essential for protecting sensitive data.

Web applications often rely on databases to store user information, and APIs (Application Programming Interfaces) to interact with other applications or retrieve additional data.

Common Web Application Vulnerabilities

Understanding common vulnerabilities helps ethical hackers identify weaknesses and recommend ways to secure web applications. Here are some of the most frequent issues encountered in web application security:

1. Cross-Site Scripting (XSS)

XSS attacks occur when attackers inject malicious scripts into a website that then executes in the browser of another user. XSS attacks can steal session cookies, redirect users, or perform unauthorized actions on behalf of the user.

- **Types of XSS**:

  o **Stored XSS**: Malicious code is saved on the server (e.g., in a comment or message), so any user who views the content executes the code.

  o **Reflected XSS**: Malicious code is embedded in a URL or form input and immediately reflected back to the user, executing if the input isn't sanitized.

  o **DOM-based XSS**: Occurs when the client-side JavaScript manipulates the DOM (Document Object Model) based on untrusted data, enabling script injection.

- **Example**:

  o **Scenario**: A comment field on a blog site doesn't sanitize input, allowing an attacker to inject a script like <script>alert('XSS');</script>. When other users view the page, the script executes.

- **Mitigation**:

  o Always sanitize and validate user inputs.

  o Use security libraries like **Content Security Policy (CSP)** to limit the scripts that can run on a site.

2. Cross-Site Request Forgery (CSRF)

CSRF tricks a user's browser into performing actions on a web application where they're already authenticated, without the user's consent. CSRF attacks exploit trust, causing users to execute unwanted actions (e.g., changing account settings) on a website without their knowledge.

- **Example**:

    o **Scenario**: A logged-in user on a banking website clicks a malicious link that submits a hidden form to transfer money from their account. Since the user is authenticated, the transfer proceeds without additional verification.

- **Mitigation**:

    o Use anti-CSRF tokens that verify each request's authenticity, ensuring that only legitimate actions are performed.

    o Require re-authentication for sensitive actions, such as password changes or money transfers.

3. SQL Injection (SQLi)

SQL injection allows attackers to manipulate SQL queries by inserting malicious SQL code into input fields. SQLi can allow attackers to retrieve, modify, or delete data, and even gain administrative access to a database.

- **Example**:

  o **Scenario**: An attacker enters ' OR 1=1-- in a login form, bypassing authentication and logging in as an admin user.

- **Mitigation**:

  o Use parameterized queries or prepared statements, which separate SQL code from data inputs, preventing SQL injection.

  o Sanitize and validate user inputs before they reach the database.

4. File Inclusion Vulnerabilities

File inclusion vulnerabilities occur when a web application dynamically loads files based on user input without proper validation. These vulnerabilities allow attackers to execute unauthorized files or view sensitive files on the server.

- **Types**:

  o **Local File Inclusion (LFI)**: Allows attackers to include files from the server's filesystem.

  o **Remote File Inclusion (RFI)**: Allows attackers to include files from an external source, potentially executing malicious code.

- **Example**:

  - **Scenario**: A web application includes files based on a URL parameter, like example.com/index.php?page=about. An attacker could replace about with ../../../etc/passwd to access sensitive files.

- **Mitigation**:

  - Limit input sources for file inclusion and sanitize all file paths.

  - Disable remote file inclusion in configuration files if it isn't needed.

5. Broken Authentication and Session Management

Weak authentication mechanisms allow attackers to impersonate users or hijack sessions, potentially accessing sensitive data or performing unauthorized actions.

- **Example**:

  - **Scenario**: A website doesn't expire session tokens after logout, allowing an attacker to reuse the token if it's leaked.

- **Mitigation**:

  - Use secure session tokens and set expiration times.

o Implement multi-factor authentication (MFA) for sensitive actions.

Example Scenarios for Practicing Web Application Security

These scenarios simulate real-world vulnerabilities, helping ethical hackers develop skills for securing web applications. Practice these exercises in a controlled environment like a local web server or a virtual lab with authorization.

1. Testing for XSS Vulnerabilities

Objective: Identify and mitigate XSS vulnerabilities in input fields.

1. **Setup**: Create a simple web page with a comment section that accepts user input.

2. **Test for XSS**: Enter <script>alert('XSS');</script> in the comment field.

    o If an alert pops up when the page reloads, the input is vulnerable to XSS.

3. **Mitigation**: Sanitize the input by removing or escaping script tags. Implement a Content Security Policy to restrict script sources.

2. Simulating a CSRF Attack

Objective: Understand how CSRF attacks work and how to implement anti-CSRF tokens.

1. **Setup**: Create a form that performs a sensitive action, such as changing a user's email address, without requiring additional verification.

2. **Test**: Create a malicious HTML file with a hidden form that submits to the same endpoint.

   o   Load the file in a browser where you're logged in to the target application. If the action is performed, the form is vulnerable.

3. **Mitigation**: Implement anti-CSRF tokens in forms that verify each request's authenticity. Require token validation to ensure only legitimate actions are performed.

3. SQL Injection Testing

Objective: Understand SQL injection and practice securing queries.

1. **Setup**: Create a login form that queries the database based on user input without parameterized queries.

2. **Test for SQLi**: Enter ' OR '1'='1 in the username field. If access is granted without a password, the form is vulnerable.

3. **Mitigation**: Implement parameterized queries or prepared statements, which treat user input as data rather than executable SQL code.

4. Testing for File Inclusion Vulnerabilities

Objective: Identify and mitigate file inclusion vulnerabilities.

1. **Setup**: Create a PHP page that dynamically includes files based on URL parameters, e.g., index.php?page=about.

2. **Test for LFI**: Modify the URL to attempt accessing system files, such as index.php?page=../../../etc/passwd.

    o   If sensitive files are displayed, the application is vulnerable to LFI.

3. **Mitigation**: Restrict file inclusions to a predefined list of safe files and sanitize file paths to prevent directory traversal.

5. Securing Session Management

Objective: Secure session management to prevent session hijacking.

1. **Setup**: Create a simple login form with session handling but no expiration or invalidation.

2. **Test**: Log in, copy the session token, and reuse it after logging out to verify if the token remains valid.

3. **Mitigation**: Set session expiration times, invalidate tokens after logout, and consider using secure cookies with the HttpOnly and Secure flags enabled.

Best Practices for Securing Web Applications

To secure web applications effectively, ethical hackers should recommend the following best practices:

1. **Input Validation and Sanitization**: Always sanitize and validate user inputs to prevent injection attacks like SQLi and XSS.

2. **Use Prepared Statements for Database Queries**: Use parameterized queries or ORM (Object Relational Mapping) libraries to separate data from SQL code.

3. **Implement Strong Authentication and Session Management**: Use secure session tokens, set expiration times, and encourage multi-factor authentication.

4. **Limit File Access and Inclusion**: Restrict file inclusions to trusted sources and disable remote file inclusions where unnecessary.

5. **Set Security Headers**: Use HTTP headers like **Content Security Policy (CSP)**, **Strict-Transport-Security (HSTS)**, and **X-Frame-Options** to mitigate vulnerabilities.

Ethical and Legal Considerations in Web Application Testing

Ethical hacking requires explicit authorization and careful adherence to privacy guidelines:

- **Scope Definition**: Clearly define which web applications, pages, or functionalities are within the testing scope.

- **Non-Destructive Testing**: Avoid actions that could corrupt data or disrupt user experience in a production environment.

- **Data Privacy**: Avoid accessing or collecting sensitive user data, and use test accounts when possible.

Document all findings and recommend solutions to enhance web application security responsibly.

Web applications present unique challenges in cybersecurity, requiring a deep understanding of common vulnerabilities and attack methods. By recognizing threats like XSS, CSRF, SQLi, and others, ethical hackers can proactively identify weaknesses and recommend security improvements.

In the next chapter, we'll cover network traffic analysis and monitoring, a critical skill for detecting suspicious activity and responding to threats in real time. Network monitoring complements vulnerability testing by providing ongoing insights into system security.

CHAPTER 14: EXPLOITING DATABASES AND SQL INJECTION

Databases are the backbone of many applications, storing essential data like user information, transaction records, and content. However, if not properly secured, databases can become a significant target for attackers. One of the most common and dangerous database-related vulnerabilities is **SQL injection (SQLi)**, where attackers manipulate SQL queries to access or modify data without authorization.

This chapter provides an overview of databases, the risks associated with insecure SQL queries, and practical exercises for understanding and mitigating SQL injection attacks.

Understanding Databases and SQL

A database is a structured collection of data, and SQL (Structured Query Language) is the standard language used to manage and manipulate this data. Databases enable applications to store, retrieve, and update data efficiently, making them essential for applications across web, mobile, and enterprise environments.

Key Database Concepts

1. **Tables**: Databases organize data into tables, each containing rows (records) and columns (fields). For example, a Users table might store information such as user_id, username, email, and password.

141

2. **Queries**: Queries are commands written in SQL to interact with the database. Common SQL commands include:

   o **SELECT**: Retrieves data from tables.

   o **INSERT**: Adds new data into tables.

   o **UPDATE**: Modifies existing data in tables.

   o **DELETE**: Removes data from tables.

3. **Primary Keys and Foreign Keys**: A primary key uniquely identifies each record in a table. Foreign keys link records between tables, establishing relationships that help maintain data integrity.

When applications send SQL queries to databases, they typically accept input from users, such as search terms or login credentials. If this input is not handled securely, it can expose the database to SQL injection attacks.

What is SQL Injection (SQLi)?

SQL injection is an attack technique where attackers manipulate user input to inject malicious SQL code into database queries. If the application does not validate or sanitize input properly, attackers can manipulate queries to bypass authentication, retrieve sensitive data, modify records, or even gain administrative control over the database.

Types of SQL Injection

1. **In-Band SQL Injection**: The attacker retrieves data directly within the application's response. This type of SQL injection is often easy to identify and exploit.

2. **Blind SQL Injection**: The application doesn't display database error messages, so attackers use true/false conditions to infer data indirectly.

3. **Out-of-Band SQL Injection**: The attacker relies on a different channel, such as HTTP requests, to extract data. This is less common but can be used when in-band or blind SQL injection is not feasible.

Common SQL Injection Techniques

1. **Authentication Bypass**: Attackers manipulate login forms to bypass authentication. For example:

   o Inputting ' OR '1'='1 in a login form might trick the database into thinking the query is true for all records.

2. **Union-Based SQL Injection**: Attackers use the UNION operator to combine results from multiple SELECT queries. This can allow attackers to retrieve additional information from other tables.

3. **Boolean-Based SQL Injection**: In blind SQL injection, attackers use true/false statements to infer data. For example, they may test different statements and check if the page content changes.

Example of a Vulnerable Query:

sql

Copy code

SELECT * FROM Users WHERE username = 'user' AND password = 'pass';

If this query is vulnerable to SQL injection, an attacker could input ' OR '1'='1 as the username, causing the query to look like:

sql

Copy code

SELECT * FROM Users WHERE username = '' OR '1'='1' AND password = 'pass';

Since '1'='1' is always true, the query may return the first record in the Users table, bypassing authentication.

Risks of Poorly Secured SQL Queries

Poorly secured SQL queries pose several risks:

1. **Data Theft**: Attackers can retrieve sensitive information, including personal data, financial records, and intellectual property.

2. **Data Manipulation**: SQL injection can allow attackers to modify or delete records, affecting data integrity.

3. **Privilege Escalation**: Attackers might gain administrative privileges, potentially compromising the entire database.

4. **Application Compromise**: SQL injection can give attackers control over the application, allowing further attacks, such as installing malware or defacing the website.

Securing SQL queries is essential for preventing these risks. Ethical hackers play a vital role in identifying SQL vulnerabilities and helping organizations implement robust defenses.

Practical Exercises for Understanding SQL Injection and Mitigations

The following exercises simulate SQL injection attacks and demonstrate how to secure SQL queries effectively. Use a test environment, such as a virtual machine or a controlled lab, for these exercises to avoid compromising real data.

Exercise 1: Basic Authentication Bypass with SQL Injection

Objective: Understand how SQL injection can be used to bypass authentication.

1. **Setup**: Create a test login form that queries a Users table for matching usernames and passwords.

   o Sample vulnerable query:

sql

SELECT * FROM Users WHERE username = 'user' AND password = 'pass';

2. **Attack**:

   o Enter ' OR '1'='1 in the username field, leaving the password blank.

   o The query should now look like:

sql

SELECT * FROM Users WHERE username = '' OR '1'='1' AND password = '';

   o This query returns a true result for the first user, potentially bypassing authentication.

3. **Mitigation**:

- o Use parameterized queries or prepared statements, which treat inputs as data rather than SQL code:

sql

SELECT * FROM Users WHERE username = ? AND password = ?;

- o This approach prevents input from being interpreted as part of the SQL code.

Exercise 2: Union-Based SQL Injection

Objective: Simulate a union-based SQL injection to retrieve unauthorized data.

1. **Setup**: Create a search form that uses the UNION operator to combine results.

   - o Sample vulnerable query:

sql

SELECT name, email FROM Users WHERE name = 'user';

2. **Attack**:

   - o Input ' UNION SELECT table_name, column_name FROM information_schema.columns-- in the search field to retrieve metadata from the database.

   - o The query might look like:

sql

SELECT name, email FROM Users WHERE name = " UNION SELECT table name, column name FROM information_ schema.columns;

- o This retrieves information about tables and columns, which an attacker can use to identify sensitive data.

3. **Mitigation**:

- o Limit the use of UNION in queries and sanitize all input fields to disallow SQL keywords.

- o Use role-based access control to restrict access to database schema metadata.

Exercise 3: Blind SQL Injection with Boolean Conditions

Objective: Understand blind SQL injection using boolean-based queries.

1. **Setup**: Create a form that doesn't display database errors or results.

2. **Attack**:

- o Input ' AND 1=1-- to test if the query returns true. Then try ' AND 1=2-- to check for false.

- o Example vulnerable query:

sql

SELECT * FROM Users WHERE username = 'user' AND 1=1--';

- o If the query returns different responses for true/false, attackers can infer information from these responses.

3. **Mitigation**:

- o Implement a query timeout and use error handling to prevent revealing database behavior.

- o Use parameterized queries to prevent input from altering query logic.

Exercise 4: Preventing SQL Injection with Parameterized Queries

Objective: Implement parameterized queries to secure database interactions.

1. **Setup**: Use the vulnerable login form from **Exercise 1**.

2. **Mitigation**:

- o Refactor the query using parameterized statements:

python

Example in Python

cursor.execute("SELECT * FROM Users WHERE username = %s AND password = %s", (username, password))

> o Test the form to verify that inputs like ' OR '1'='1 no longer bypass authentication.

Parameterized queries treat user inputs as data, preventing them from being executed as part of the SQL statement.

Best Practices for Securing SQL Queries

To protect applications and databases from SQL injection, ethical hackers can recommend these best practices:

1. **Use Parameterized Queries**: Parameterized queries separate SQL code from user input, preventing inputs from being interpreted as SQL commands.

2. **Limit Database Permissions**: Use the principle of least privilege. Only give applications access to the tables and actions necessary for their functionality, reducing the risk of damage if a breach occurs.

3. **Sanitize and Validate Input**: Always sanitize and validate user inputs, checking for illegal characters or keywords that could be used in SQL injection.

4. **Use ORM Libraries**: Object Relational Mapping (ORM) libraries, such as SQLAlchemy or Django ORM, abstract SQL queries, making it harder to introduce SQL injection.

5. **Regularly Update and Patch Databases**: Database vendors frequently release security patches. Keeping databases up to date ensures protection against newly discovered vulnerabilities.

Ethical and Legal Considerations in SQL Injection Testing

Testing for SQL injection vulnerabilities must be conducted ethically and responsibly:

- **Obtain Authorization**: Only test for SQL injection on databases and applications where you have explicit permission.

- **Limit Testing Scope**: Focus on authorized input fields or test environments, avoiding unintended damage to live systems.

- **Data Privacy**: Avoid accessing sensitive information unless explicitly permitted, and ensure that any test data retrieved is handled according to privacy guidelines.

Document findings and provide recommendations that prioritize both security and system stability.

SQL injection remains one of the most prevalent and dangerous web application vulnerabilities. By understanding how SQL injection works and practicing mitigation techniques, ethical hackers can identify potential risks and help organizations secure their databases against unauthorized access and data manipulation.

In the next chapter, we'll delve into network traffic analysis and monitoring. This skill is crucial for detecting suspicious activity, analyzing potential breaches, and responding to threats in real time. Network monitoring complements vulnerability testing by providing ongoing insights into network security.

Chapter 15: Malware Basics and Countermeasures

Malware, short for malicious software, refers to any program or code intentionally designed to disrupt, damage, or gain unauthorized access to systems. Malware remains a significant threat in cybersecurity, with new variants emerging daily. Understanding how malware operates, the types of malware, and effective countermeasures are crucial for ethical hackers to protect systems and respond to infections.

In this chapter, we'll explore common types of malware, provide an overview of malware analysis, and discuss detection and prevention techniques. We'll also cover basic malware analysis exercises in controlled environments to help ethical hackers understand how malware operates and is detected.

Types of Malware

Malware comes in various forms, each with unique characteristics and attack vectors. The most common types include viruses, worms, trojans, and ransomware.

1. Viruses

- **Description**: A virus is malicious code attached to a legitimate program or file. It spreads when the infected file is opened or executed, often replicating itself and infecting other files on the system.

- **Impact**: Viruses can corrupt files, slow down systems, or delete data. Some viruses are relatively harmless, while others are highly destructive.

- **Example**: The Melissa virus, one of the earliest email-based viruses, spread via infected email attachments and caused widespread disruptions.

2. Worms

- **Description**: Worms are standalone malware that can self-replicate and spread independently. Unlike viruses, worms don't require a host file to operate, which makes them highly contagious.

- **Impact**: Worms can quickly propagate across networks, consuming bandwidth, overloading servers, and delivering additional malicious payloads.

- **Example**: The SQL Slammer worm exploited a vulnerability in Microsoft SQL Server, spreading rapidly across the internet and causing widespread network slowdowns.

3. Trojans

- **Description**: Trojans disguise themselves as legitimate software, tricking users into installing them. Once installed, they create backdoors or steal sensitive information.

- **Impact**: Trojans allow attackers to control infected systems, access sensitive data, or install other malware. Some trojans, known as Remote Access Trojans (RATs), give attackers full control over the infected device.

- **Example**: The Emotet trojan masquerades as legitimate email attachments, allowing attackers to steal data or distribute other malware.

4. Ransomware

- **Description**: Ransomware encrypts files or locks users out of their systems, demanding a ransom for access. It typically spreads via phishing emails, malicious downloads, or unpatched vulnerabilities.

- **Impact**: Ransomware can disrupt entire networks and cost organizations millions in downtime and ransom payments.

- **Example**: The WannaCry ransomware attack exploited a vulnerability in Windows systems, spreading globally and affecting organizations, hospitals, and government agencies.

How Malware Infects Systems

Malware employs various methods to infect systems and evade detection. Understanding these methods helps ethical hackers identify and protect against threats. Some common infection techniques include:

1. **Social Engineering**: Attackers use social engineering tactics, such as phishing emails or fake software updates, to trick users into downloading malware.

2. **Exploiting Vulnerabilities**: Malware often exploits unpatched software vulnerabilities, allowing attackers to install malware without user interaction.

3. **Drive-By Downloads**: Certain websites deliver malware through drive-by downloads, where users download malicious files without realizing it.

4. **Malicious Attachments**: Email attachments, often disguised as legitimate documents or links, are a popular method for delivering malware to unsuspecting users.

Basic Malware Analysis

Malware analysis is the process of studying malware to understand its behavior, impact, and techniques. Ethical hackers and security professionals analyze malware to identify indicators of compromise (IOCs), improve detection, and develop effective countermeasures.

Types of Malware Analysis

1. **Static Analysis**: Static analysis involves examining malware code without executing it. This can reveal information about its functions, libraries, and structure. While basic, static analysis can identify key characteristics like strings, metadata, and embedded resources.

2. **Dynamic Analysis**: Dynamic analysis involves running malware in a controlled environment to observe its behavior in real time. This method reveals details such as network connections, file system changes, and registry modifications.

3. **Behavioral Analysis**: Behavioral analysis combines static and dynamic analysis to study malware's interaction with the system. This method identifies patterns and tactics that malware uses to avoid detection.

Tools for Malware Analysis

- **Static Analysis Tools**:

  - **Strings**: Identifies readable text in malware files, such as URLs or commands.

  - **IDA Pro**: A popular disassembler and debugger that reveals low-level instructions in the malware code.

- **Dynamic Analysis Tools**:

- ○ **Wireshark**: Monitors network traffic to detect malicious connections.

- ○ **Process Monitor (ProcMon)**: Tracks file system, registry, and process activity on Windows, revealing changes made by malware.

- ○ **Sandbox Environments (e.g., Cuckoo Sandbox)**: Isolated environments that safely execute malware to analyze behavior.

Note: Always analyze malware in a controlled, isolated environment, such as a virtual machine, to prevent accidental infections.

Hands-On Exercises: Malware Analysis and Detection

These exercises are intended for controlled lab environments or virtual machines to understand malware behavior without compromising real systems. Ensure all analysis is conducted in isolated, non-networked environments.

Exercise 1: Basic Static Analysis

Objective: Extract information from malware without executing it.

1. **Setup**: Obtain a sample benign malware file (such as a harmless text-based virus example).

2. **Use the strings command**:

o Run strings on the malware file to identify readable text:

bash

strings malware_sample.exe

o **Observe**: Note any URLs, IP addresses, suspicious commands, or encoded strings. These may indicate the malware's functionality, such as downloading files or connecting to command-and-control (C2) servers.

3. **Use a Hex Editor**:

o Open the file with a hex editor to analyze its structure and identify patterns.

Outcome: This analysis helps identify initial indicators of compromise and the general purpose of the malware.

Exercise 2: Dynamic Analysis with Process Monitor

Objective: Observe real-time system changes made by malware.

1. **Setup**: Launch a virtual machine with Process Monitor (ProcMon) installed.

2. **Run Process Monitor**:

o Start ProcMon to monitor registry, file, and process changes.

3. **Execute the Malware Sample**:

o Run the malware sample in the virtual machine and observe any new processes, registry changes, or file modifications in ProcMon.

4. **Analyze Results**:

o Check for suspicious changes, such as attempts to modify startup files, create new processes, or alter the registry.

Outcome: Dynamic analysis reveals behavioral indicators and provides a clear view of how malware interacts with the system.

Exercise 3: Network Traffic Analysis with Wireshark

Objective: Capture and analyze network traffic to identify malicious connections.

1. **Setup**: Launch a virtual machine with Wireshark installed.

2. **Monitor Network Traffic**:

o Open Wireshark, select the network interface, and start capturing packets.

3. **Execute the Malware Sample**:

o Run the malware sample and observe the traffic in Wireshark.

4. **Analyze Network Behavior**:

o Look for unusual connections, such as repeated attempts to contact external IP addresses, download commands, or connections to known malicious domains.

Outcome: Network analysis identifies potential communication with C2 servers and data exfiltration attempts, which are key indicators of malicious activity.

Detection and Prevention Techniques

1. **Antivirus and Endpoint Detection and Response (EDR)**: Antivirus software and EDR solutions scan systems for known malware signatures and suspicious behavior. EDR solutions provide advanced threat detection, endpoint isolation, and response capabilities.

2. **Firewall and Intrusion Detection Systems (IDS)**: Firewalls control incoming and outgoing traffic, while IDS monitors for unusual patterns. Configuring firewalls and IDS with malware-specific signatures improves network security.

3. **Behavior-Based Detection**: Behavior-based systems identify malware based on its actions rather than its signature. This method is effective for detecting unknown or polymorphic malware, which changes code to evade signature-based detection.

4. **Regular Software Updates and Patch Management**: Many malware types exploit unpatched vulnerabilities. Keeping systems up to date reduces the risk of infection.

5. **User Awareness and Training**: Educating users on malware risks, such as avoiding phishing emails or suspicious downloads, is one of the most effective prevention methods.

Countermeasures for Specific Malware Types

1. **Viruses**:

   o Use antivirus software to scan and remove known viruses.

   o Enable system restore points, which allow recovery to a previous state in case of infection.

2. **Worms**:

   o Isolate infected systems to prevent network spread.

o Regularly update systems and network equipment to close vulnerabilities that worms might exploit.

3. **Trojans**:

   o Use application whitelisting to limit executable files to trusted sources.

   o Monitor for suspicious remote connections that may indicate backdoors.

4. **Ransomware**:

   o Maintain regular, offline backups to ensure data recovery without paying ransoms.

   o Implement access controls and limit permissions to reduce the impact of ransomware infections.

Ethical and Legal Considerations in Malware Analysis

Malware analysis must be conducted responsibly to ensure the safety of systems and users:

- **Isolate Malware Samples**: Always analyze malware in isolated environments, such as virtual machines or sandboxed setups, to prevent accidental spread.

- **Avoid Real-World Infection**: Refrain from testing malware on live or production systems.

- **Adhere to Legal Guidelines**: Handling malware, even in a lab, may be restricted by local regulations. Ensure compliance with relevant laws and permissions.

Document findings carefully, report vulnerabilities to relevant parties, and provide actionable recommendations to enhance system security.

Understanding the fundamentals of malware, from viruses to ransomware, enables ethical hackers to detect, analyze, and prevent malware attacks. Through hands-on exercises and analysis techniques, ethical hackers can uncover how malware operates and help organizations implement robust defenses.

In the next chapter, we'll discuss network traffic analysis and monitoring in more depth. This skill is essential for detecting malware, identifying suspicious activity, and responding to network threats in real-time. Network monitoring complements malware analysis by providing ongoing insights into system security.

CHAPTER 16: NETWORK SNIFFING AND TRAFFIC ANALYSIS

Network sniffing and traffic analysis are critical skills in cybersecurity, enabling ethical hackers and security professionals to monitor and interpret network activity. By capturing and analyzing packets, ethical hackers can detect suspicious behavior, locate vulnerabilities, and even uncover instances where sensitive data is being transmitted insecurely. This chapter introduces network sniffing, packet analysis tools like Wireshark, and provides a real-world example to demonstrate how packet analysis can reveal sensitive information.

What is Network Sniffing?

Network sniffing is the process of intercepting and capturing data packets as they travel across a network. Ethical hackers and network administrators use sniffing to monitor traffic, troubleshoot issues, and identify security risks.

Types of Network Sniffing

1. **Passive Sniffing**: Passive sniffing involves monitoring network traffic without altering or interacting with the data. This technique is common in networks with a hub setup, where all data packets are visible to all connected devices.

2. **Active Sniffing**: Active sniffing requires interacting with the network to capture specific packets. This method is often

used on switched networks, where packets are directed to specific devices, making passive sniffing challenging. Active sniffing can involve techniques like ARP (Address Resolution Protocol) spoofing to intercept targeted packets.

Network sniffing can reveal a wealth of information, from IP addresses and protocols used to details about data and services. However, it requires strict authorization and ethical boundaries, as intercepting network data without consent is illegal.

Understanding Packet Analysis

Packet analysis involves examining captured data packets to gain insights into network activity, application performance, and potential security threats. Ethical hackers and network administrators use packet analysis to:

1. **Identify Suspicious Activity**: Analyze packets for unusual traffic patterns that might indicate malware, unauthorized access, or network reconnaissance.

2. **Troubleshoot Network Issues**: Detect bottlenecks, dropped packets, or misconfigurations that affect network performance.

3. **Ensure Data Security**: Check if sensitive data, such as passwords or financial information, is being transmitted in plaintext.

Each packet contains headers (metadata about the packet) and payloads (actual data), allowing analysts to view details such as the packet's source and destination, protocol, and contents.

Packet Analysis Tools

Several tools allow ethical hackers to capture and analyze network packets. Wireshark is one of the most widely used and powerful tools, but other options are available depending on the needs and environment.

1. Wireshark

Wireshark is a free, open-source packet analyzer with a user-friendly interface. It captures live traffic, decodes packet data, and provides filtering options to isolate specific types of data.

- **Features**:

    o Real-time packet capture and detailed analysis.

    o Filters to sort by IP addresses, protocols, ports, and more.

    o Visualization tools to track packet flow and identify patterns.

- **Common Use Cases**:

- o Detecting insecure protocols (e.g., unencrypted HTTP).

- o Troubleshooting connectivity issues by analyzing packet flow.

- o Identifying unusual traffic patterns that indicate attacks.

2. tcpdump

tcpdump is a command-line packet capture tool that's often used on Linux systems. It's lightweight and effective for quick packet analysis and capturing traffic for later analysis in Wireshark.

- **Features**:

  - o Command-line interface suitable for scripting and automation.

  - o Can capture and save packets for analysis in other tools like Wireshark.

- **Common Use Cases**:

  - o Quick network diagnostics and analysis in terminal-based environments.

  - o Packet capture for long-term monitoring in scripted setups.

3. TShark

TShark is the command-line version of Wireshark, providing similar functionality for environments where a graphical interface isn't available.

- **Features**:

  - Allows all Wireshark filters and features but runs from the command line.

  - Can save captures to files for later analysis in Wireshark.

- **Common Use Cases**:

  - Detailed analysis in remote or terminal-only environments.

  - Automation of Wireshark capabilities in scripts.

Note: These tools should only be used in authorized environments to ensure ethical practices and compliance with privacy regulations.

Real-World Example: Revealing Sensitive Data through Packet Analysis

To understand how packet analysis can uncover sensitive information, let's look at a scenario where insecure data transmission reveals critical information about users.

Scenario: Capturing Unencrypted Credentials

1. **Setup**: Assume we're analyzing a corporate network to ensure employees aren't using insecure connections. During the analysis, we focus on HTTP traffic, as HTTP transmits data in plaintext.

2. **Capturing Packets with Wireshark**:

   o Open Wireshark, select the appropriate network interface, and begin capturing packets.

   o Set a filter to capture only HTTP traffic:

plaintext

http

   o Start browsing a website that uses HTTP (unencrypted), such as an internal test website, and enter login credentials.

3. **Analyzing Packets**:

   o After stopping the capture, look for packets containing the POST request to the login page.

   o Right-click the packet, select "Follow" > "HTTP Stream," to see the entire request and response data in sequence.

o **Observation**: Wireshark displays the HTTP POST request, which includes login credentials in plaintext, as HTTP doesn't encrypt data.

4. **Outcome**:

o This example reveals sensitive data (username and password) transmitted in plaintext. Ethical hackers can use this information to recommend transitioning from HTTP to HTTPS, ensuring data security.

Note: This exercise should be performed only in a test environment where it's safe and authorized to capture data. Never intercept data without explicit permission.

Hands-On Exercises: Network Sniffing and Packet Analysis

The following exercises help ethical hackers practice network sniffing and packet analysis using Wireshark in controlled environments.

Exercise 1: Basic Packet Capture and Filtering in Wireshark

Objective: Learn the basics of capturing packets and filtering traffic for specific types of data.

1. **Setup**: Open Wireshark and select your network interface (e.g., eth0, wlan0).

2. **Start Capture**:

      o   Click "Start" to begin capturing packets.

3. **Filter by Protocol**:

      o   Enter "http" in the filter bar to view only HTTP traffic.

4. **Stop Capture**:

      o   Stop the capture after browsing an HTTP website.

5. **Analyze Packets**:

      o   Select an HTTP GET or POST request, and view details like source/destination IP addresses, port numbers, and request content.

Outcome: This exercise helps you practice using Wireshark filters and understanding HTTP packet structure.

Exercise 2: Analyzing DNS Traffic

Objective: Capture and analyze DNS queries to understand domain resolution and identify potential DNS-based attacks.

1. **Setup**: Open Wireshark and begin a new capture.

2. **Filter by DNS**:

      o   Enter "dns" in the filter bar.

3. **Generate DNS Traffic**:

o   In a browser, visit multiple websites to generate DNS requests.

4. **Analyze DNS Queries**:

o   Look for DNS requests and responses, noting the resolved IP addresses and requested domains.

5. **Identify Patterns**:

o   If performing this in a lab, analyze requests to detect unusual domains or rapid requests, which may indicate malicious activity like DNS tunneling.

Outcome: This exercise familiarizes you with DNS traffic, helping you recognize normal DNS queries versus potentially malicious requests.

Exercise 3: Detecting Suspicious Traffic with Wireshark

Objective: Identify abnormal traffic patterns that could indicate a network attack, such as a Distributed Denial of Service (DDoS) attack.

1. **Setup**: Open Wireshark and start capturing packets on your network.

2. **Generate Traffic** (optional): Use a testing tool to simulate high-traffic requests to your test environment.

3. **Analyze ICMP Traffic**:

   o Filter for ICMP (ping) traffic by entering icmp in the filter bar.

4. **Look for Patterns**:

   o Observe the frequency and volume of ICMP requests. If you see an unusually high volume of pings, it may indicate a DDoS or network reconnaissance.

Outcome: This exercise helps you understand how packet analysis can reveal suspicious activity patterns in network traffic.

Detecting and Preventing Sniffing Attacks

Ethical hackers should recommend countermeasures to protect networks from unauthorized sniffing and data exposure:

1. **Use Encryption (HTTPS, SSL/TLS)**: Encrypted protocols like HTTPS ensure that data is unreadable even if captured. Sensitive data, such as login credentials and financial information, should always be encrypted.

2. **Implement Network Segmentation**: Isolate sensitive networks or VLANs (Virtual Local Area Networks) to reduce the risk of unauthorized access to critical data.

3. **Use Secure Wi-Fi (WPA3)**: Use strong encryption standards like WPA3 for wireless networks to prevent unauthorized sniffing.

4. **Enable Switch Port Security**: Implement port security on network switches to prevent unauthorized devices from capturing packets.

5. **Regularly Monitor Network Traffic**: Regular traffic analysis helps detect unusual patterns and ensures that unauthorized sniffing tools are identified and removed quickly.

Ethical and Legal Considerations in Network Sniffing

Network sniffing and packet analysis require strict adherence to ethical and legal boundaries:

- **Authorization**: Obtain explicit permission before capturing or analyzing network traffic.

- **Limit Scope**: Capture only the necessary data, focusing on authorized networks and IP addresses.

- **Data Privacy**: Avoid capturing or storing sensitive data like user credentials or personal information. Use anonymized data whenever possible.

- **Reporting and Documentation**: Document all findings responsibly, providing recommendations to enhance network security without compromising user privacy.

Network sniffing and traffic analysis are valuable skills that help ethical hackers detect vulnerabilities, identify suspicious activities, and protect data from unauthorized access. By using tools like Wireshark and practicing packet analysis techniques, ethical hackers can provide actionable insights that enhance network security.

In the next chapter, we'll cover incident response and remediation, discussing how ethical hackers and cybersecurity teams can respond to detected threats, contain potential damage, and restore systems to a secure state. Incident response is a critical component of cybersecurity, bridging detection and prevention efforts.

CHAPTER 17: INTRODUCTION TO PENETRATION TESTING

Penetration testing, often called "pen testing," is a systematic process in which ethical hackers simulate real-world attacks to identify security weaknesses in systems, networks, and applications. The goal is to find and remediate vulnerabilities before they can be exploited by malicious actors. Penetration testing follows a structured approach, ensuring tests are thorough, legally compliant, and ethically conducted.

In this chapter, we'll discuss the structure of a penetration test, covering each phase from planning to reporting. We'll also explore the ethical and legal distinctions between penetration testing and malicious hacking, clarifying why authorization and compliance are vital for ethical hackers.

What is Penetration Testing?

Penetration testing is a controlled assessment where ethical hackers, often called penetration testers or pen testers, simulate cyberattacks on an organization's systems to identify vulnerabilities. Unlike malicious hacking, penetration testing is conducted with the explicit permission of the organization and follows a defined scope, ensuring it remains ethical and legal.

Penetration testing helps organizations:

- Identify and fix vulnerabilities in their systems, applications, and networks.

- Test the effectiveness of existing security measures.

- Improve employee security awareness and incident response readiness.

- Comply with industry standards and regulations, such as PCI-DSS, HIPAA, and ISO/IEC 27001.

Structure of a Penetration Test

A typical penetration test consists of four main phases: planning, scanning, exploitation, and reporting. Each phase serves a specific purpose, building on the results of the previous steps to create a comprehensive security assessment.

1. Planning and Preparation

Planning is the foundation of a successful penetration test. In this phase, the ethical hacker works closely with the organization to define the scope, objectives, and rules of engagement. This phase ensures that all parties agree on the details of the test, including legal and operational boundaries.

- **Defining Scope**: The scope specifies which systems, applications, or networks are included in the test. It also clarifies the level of access allowed (e.g., whether testers start as unauthenticated external users or as internal network users).

- **Setting Objectives**: Objectives define the test's goals, such as identifying critical vulnerabilities, assessing network resilience, or testing employee response to phishing.

- **Rules of Engagement**: These are the agreed-upon guidelines for the test, including authorized testing methods, prohibited actions, and escalation procedures if critical vulnerabilities are identified.

- **Legal Authorization**: The organization grants written authorization for the test, protecting the ethical hacker from legal consequences. Without permission, any hacking attempt is illegal.

Example: In a web application penetration test, the scope might include testing the app for SQL injection, XSS vulnerabilities, and weak authentication methods, but exclude testing on production databases or user data.

2. Scanning and Reconnaissance

In this phase, penetration testers gather as much information as possible about the target systems. Reconnaissance and scanning help identify potential entry points and vulnerabilities.

- **Passive Reconnaissance**: Gathering publicly available information without interacting directly with the target. Passive methods include DNS lookups, WHOIS searches, and social media analysis.

- **Active Reconnaissance**: Directly interacting with the target systems to gather detailed information. This might include port scanning, service enumeration, and vulnerability scanning.

- **Tools**: Pen testers use tools like Nmap for port scanning, Nessus for vulnerability scanning, and Shodan for finding exposed assets.

Example: A pen tester might use Nmap to scan for open ports on a web server and use Nessus to identify software vulnerabilities associated with the services running on those ports.

3. Exploitation

Exploitation is the phase where ethical hackers attempt to exploit identified vulnerabilities. The goal is to determine if the vulnerabilities can be used to gain unauthorized access, escalate privileges, or compromise the system in other ways. This phase must be carefully controlled to avoid disrupting services or causing unintended damage.

- **Controlled Exploitation**: Ethical hackers typically avoid highly destructive or risky exploits and focus on proving the vulnerability exists without damaging data or systems.

- **Post-Exploitation**: Once access is gained, pen testers may examine what information or resources they can access, such as sensitive files, databases, or network segments. However, ethical boundaries are maintained, ensuring sensitive data isn't copied or viewed unnecessarily.

- **Tools**: Tools like Metasploit, Burp Suite, and Hydra are commonly used to test for SQL injection, cross-site scripting, brute-force attacks, and other vulnerabilities.

Example: If a tester finds a SQL injection vulnerability in a login form, they may exploit it to retrieve limited information, such as a list of usernames, to demonstrate the flaw without accessing or altering sensitive user data.

4. Reporting

The reporting phase is where the penetration tester documents their findings, detailing identified vulnerabilities, exploitation methods, and recommendations for remediation. The report serves as a roadmap for the organization to improve its security posture.

- **Executive Summary**: A high-level overview of the test's objectives, findings, and recommendations, written in non-technical language for management and decision-makers.

- **Detailed Findings**: A technical section detailing each vulnerability, how it was discovered, potential impacts, and exploitation methods. Each finding includes risk ratings, such as low, medium, high, or critical.

- **Remediation Recommendations**: Specific advice on how to mitigate each vulnerability, including patching instructions, configuration changes, or user education.

- **Evidence**: Screenshots, log files, and output from tools may be included as evidence to support findings and recommendations.

Example: The report might include a high-severity SQL injection vulnerability, detailing how the tester exploited it to access a test database and recommending the use of parameterized queries to prevent SQL injection.

Penetration Testing vs. Malicious Hacking

While penetration testing and hacking both involve breaking into systems, there are critical differences in terms of purpose, legality, and ethical considerations:

Purpose

- **Penetration Testing**: The purpose of penetration testing is to identify and fix security weaknesses in a controlled, authorized environment. Ethical hackers simulate real attacks to help organizations improve their defenses.

- **Malicious Hacking**: Malicious hacking is unauthorized and illegal. Attackers break into systems to steal data, cause disruption, or profit from the breach, often without regard for the consequences.

Legality and Authorization

- **Penetration Testing**: Ethical hackers have legal authorization from the organization to perform penetration testing. A formal agreement, typically called a "Rules of Engagement," outlines what can and cannot be done, providing legal protection for both parties.

- **Malicious Hacking**: Hacking without permission is illegal, as it violates cybersecurity laws. Unauthorized access, data theft, and tampering with systems can result in criminal charges and penalties.

Ethical Boundaries

- **Penetration Testing**: Ethical hackers follow strict boundaries, only testing within the authorized scope and avoiding sensitive data. The objective is to identify vulnerabilities without causing harm.

- **Malicious Hacking**: Malicious hackers often ignore ethical boundaries, prioritizing profit or personal gain over security. They may deliberately steal or damage data, spread malware, or cause other harm.

Example: A penetration tester might identify a vulnerability that allows access to sensitive files but will avoid opening or copying them. In contrast, a malicious hacker would exploit the vulnerability to steal or sell the data, regardless of privacy laws or ethical concerns.

Types of Penetration Testing

Penetration tests vary based on their scope, objectives, and level of access. Common types include:

1. **Black Box Testing**: Testers have no prior knowledge of the target environment, simulating an external attack. This method often includes discovering and exploiting public-facing vulnerabilities, such as in web applications.

2. **White Box Testing**: Testers have full knowledge of the target, including network diagrams, system configurations, and source code. White box testing is thorough and effective for identifying deeper security issues.

3. **Gray Box Testing**: Testers have limited knowledge, simulating an internal attacker or a compromised user. This approach combines the realistic perspective of black box testing with the depth of white box testing.

4. **Social Engineering Testing**: Social engineering tests target human vulnerabilities, testing how employees respond to phishing, pretexting, or physical security tests.

5. **Network Penetration Testing**: Focuses on the organization's network, assessing firewalls, routers, and network services for vulnerabilities.

6. **Web Application Penetration Testing**: Specifically targets web applications, testing for issues like SQL injection, cross-site scripting (XSS), and session management vulnerabilities.

Best Practices for Conducting a Penetration Test

To ensure an effective and ethical penetration test, ethical hackers should follow these best practices:

1. **Define Clear Objectives and Scope**: Work with the organization to establish a well-defined scope, focusing on high-risk areas and critical systems.

2. **Obtain Written Authorization**: Always secure legal authorization before testing to avoid legal repercussions and ensure all parties are informed.

3. **Follow a Methodical Approach**: Structure the test into planning, scanning, exploitation, and reporting phases, ensuring each step builds upon the previous findings.

4. **Maintain Documentation**: Document findings throughout the test, including evidence of vulnerabilities and actions taken. This helps ensure transparency and accuracy in the final report.

5. **Respect Ethical Boundaries**: Avoid testing beyond the authorized scope, refrain from accessing sensitive data, and prioritize system integrity and privacy.

6. **Provide Actionable Remediation**: Offer clear, actionable recommendations in the final report, enabling the organization to mitigate identified risks effectively.

Ethical and Legal Considerations in Penetration Testing

Ethical and legal considerations are central to penetration testing. Ethical hackers must:

- **Obtain Explicit Consent**: Written authorization is mandatory to ensure all parties understand the test's purpose, scope, and limitations.

- **Respect Confidentiality**: Treat all data and findings confidentially, avoiding exposure of sensitive information and complying with data privacy regulations.

- **Follow Industry Standards**: Use established frameworks, such as the Penetration Testing Execution Standard (PTES) or NIST guidelines, to maintain a professional and consistent approach.

- **Document Findings Responsibly**: Provide clear, factual reporting without exaggerating vulnerabilities or downplaying risks. Recommendations should be practical and prioritize the organization's security needs.

Penetration testing is a valuable and systematic approach for identifying and mitigating vulnerabilities in systems, applications, and networks. By following structured phases—planning, scanning, exploitation, and reporting—ethical hackers can provide a thorough security assessment that helps organizations strengthen their defenses. Unlike malicious hacking, penetration testing is authorized, ethical, and focuses on improving security rather than causing harm.

In the next chapter, we'll explore post-attack analysis and incident response, examining how ethical hackers and security teams respond to identified threats, contain damage, and restore system integrity. Incident response is crucial for minimizing the impact of security incidents and protecting organizations from future attacks.

CHAPTER 18: REPORTING AND DOCUMENTING VULNERABILITIES

One of the most critical phases in a penetration test is reporting and documenting findings. An effective vulnerability report is more than a list of issues; it's a comprehensive document that clearly communicates security weaknesses, their implications, and actionable recommendations for remediation. The goal of vulnerability reporting is to ensure that the client understands the identified risks and has clear guidance on addressing them.

In this chapter, we'll explore how to create clear, actionable reports, discuss the components of a well-structured vulnerability report, and highlight examples of good versus bad reporting practices.

Why Reporting is Essential in Penetration Testing

The report is the tangible outcome of a penetration test and serves several purposes:

1. **Communicating Findings**: The report explains each vulnerability, its impact, and evidence supporting the findings.

2. **Providing Remediation Guidance**: By including actionable recommendations, the report enables the client to address vulnerabilities effectively.

3. **Demonstrating Compliance**: In regulated industries, a well-documented report may satisfy compliance requirements and show that the organization has taken steps to secure its systems.

4. **Building Trust and Transparency**: A clear report shows professionalism and builds trust, demonstrating that the penetration test was conducted thoroughly and ethically.

Structure of a Vulnerability Report

A well-structured vulnerability report typically includes the following sections:

1. **Executive Summary**

   o A high-level overview of the test's objectives, findings, and overall security posture. This section is written in non-technical language for stakeholders, such as executives and management, who may not be familiar with technical details.

   o **Content**: Scope of the test, key findings, risk summary, and high-priority recommendations.

2. **Methodology**

   o A brief description of the methods and tools used during the penetration test, following industry standards (e.g., PTES or OWASP) where applicable. This section assures clients that the test was conducted using reputable and systematic practices.

- o **Content**: Reconnaissance, scanning, exploitation techniques, and tools used, along with a description of the testing phases.

3. **Detailed Findings**

- o A technical breakdown of each identified vulnerability, including severity levels, evidence, and recommended solutions. Findings should be clearly documented and organized by priority.

- o **Content**:

  - ▪ **Vulnerability Description**: Explanation of the vulnerability, including background information for context.

  - ▪ **Impact**: Potential consequences if the vulnerability is exploited.

  - ▪ **Evidence**: Screenshots, logs, or tool outputs that validate the finding.

- **Risk Level**: Severity rating (e.g., critical, high, medium, low) based on the potential impact and likelihood of exploitation.

- **Recommendations**: Actionable steps to mitigate or remediate the issue.

4. Conclusion and Recommendations

o   A summary of the overall security posture based on the findings, along with general recommendations for strengthening security beyond the identified vulnerabilities.

o   **Content**: Insights into areas that may need more focus (e.g., network segmentation, patch management) and suggestions for continuous improvement.

5. Appendices (Optional)

o   Additional information, such as a glossary of technical terms, detailed command outputs, or references to security standards, that can provide further context for the reader.

Examples of Good vs. Bad Reporting Practices

Writing a high-quality report requires attention to clarity, accuracy, and detail. Here are some examples of good versus bad practices in reporting:

1. Clarity in Description

- **Bad Practice**: "The system has a vulnerability that could be exploited by attackers."

  o **Issue**: This statement is vague, lacks specifics, and doesn't explain the risk or the type of vulnerability.

- **Good Practice**: "The application's login form is vulnerable to SQL injection, which could allow an attacker to bypass authentication and gain unauthorized access to user data."

  o **Why This is Better**: The statement is specific, naming the vulnerability (SQL injection) and explaining the potential impact (bypass authentication).

2. Actionable Remediation

- **Bad Practice**: "The company should secure its systems."

  o **Issue**: This recommendation is too broad and doesn't provide specific guidance.

- **Good Practice**: "To mitigate the SQL injection vulnerability, implement parameterized queries in the login form to prevent user input from being treated as SQL code."

  o **Why This is Better**: This recommendation is precise, explaining the exact steps (use of parameterized queries) needed to remediate the vulnerability.

3. Evidence and Validation

- **Bad Practice**: "An XSS vulnerability was found in the search field."

  o **Issue**: No evidence is provided, and there's no indication of how the vulnerability was discovered.

- **Good Practice**: "An XSS vulnerability was identified in the search field. The tester injected <script>alert('XSS');</script> as input, which was executed on the page, demonstrating a lack of input sanitization. (See screenshot in Figure 1)."

  o **Why This is Better**: This finding is backed by evidence, including details of the test input and a screenshot, validating the discovery.

4. Consistent Severity Ratings

- **Bad Practice**: Arbitrarily assigning severity ratings without context.

- **Good Practice**: Assign severity based on industry standards, such as CVSS (Common Vulnerability Scoring System), and explain the rationale. For instance, "The SQL injection vulnerability was rated 'high' because it allows unauthorized access to sensitive data and is relatively easy to exploit."

  - o **Why This is Better**: This approach provides a clear rationale for severity ratings, helping stakeholders understand the prioritization of issues.

5. Language and Tone

- **Bad Practice**: Using overly technical jargon or alarmist language that may confuse or frighten non-technical stakeholders.

- **Good Practice**: Write in a balanced, factual tone, using language that's accessible to both technical and non-technical readers. Avoid unnecessary jargon and use plain language where possible.

  - o **Example**: "The identified vulnerabilities can lead to unauthorized data access if left unaddressed.

Implementing the recommended fixes will help strengthen the security posture and reduce risk."

- o **Why This is Better**: This tone is reassuring, professional, and focused on improvement rather than inducing fear.

Sample Vulnerability Report Excerpt

Here's an example of how to write a specific vulnerability entry in a penetration testing report:

Vulnerability: SQL Injection in Login Form

- **Description**: The login form is vulnerable to SQL injection. Unsanitized input allows attackers to manipulate SQL queries, potentially bypassing authentication and accessing user information.

- **Impact**: If exploited, this vulnerability allows unauthorized access to the application, putting user data at risk and compromising account security.

- **Evidence**:

  - o **Test Input**: Username: ' OR '1'='1

  - o **Result**: The SQL injection input allowed the tester to bypass authentication and gain access to the application as an authorized user. (See screenshot in Figure 1.)

- **Severity**: High

- **Recommendations**:

  o **Use Parameterized Queries**: Modify the login query to use parameterized queries, ensuring that user input is treated as data rather than SQL code.

  o **Input Validation**: Implement server-side input validation to filter out special characters commonly used in SQL injection.

  o **Testing**: Regularly test inputs for injection vulnerabilities as part of application maintenance.

Best Practices for Effective Vulnerability Reporting

1. **Use a Standardized Format**: Maintain a consistent format across all findings to help readers quickly understand each vulnerability, its impact, and the recommended actions.

2. **Tailor Language for the Audience**: Write the executive summary for a non-technical audience, and provide more technical details in the detailed findings section for IT and security teams.

3. **Be Objective and Professional**: Avoid exaggerated claims, alarmist language, or overly technical jargon. Aim to communicate risks and recommendations in a balanced and constructive manner.

4. **Prioritize Vulnerabilities by Risk**: Use a recognized risk rating method (e.g., CVSS) to classify vulnerabilities. Prioritize critical and high-risk findings in the executive summary to guide stakeholders' focus.

5. **Make Recommendations Actionable and Specific**: Provide precise, practical guidance for each vulnerability, ensuring that the client has clear steps to address the findings.

6. **Use Visual Aids**: Include screenshots, flow diagrams, or tables where applicable to clarify complex information or validate findings with visual evidence.

7. **Ensure Accuracy and Double-Check Findings**: Verify all findings before including them in the report. Incorrect findings or false positives can damage trust and may result in wasted resources.

Common Pitfalls in Vulnerability Reporting

1. **Omitting Evidence**: Failing to provide evidence weakens the credibility of the findings and makes it difficult for the client to validate the issues.

2. **Using Ambiguous Language**: Vague descriptions or recommendations leave the client uncertain about the actual risk and what actions to take.

3. **Lack of Actionable Remediation**: General suggestions like "Improve security" or "Patch vulnerabilities" don't provide clear guidance. Recommendations should be practical and specific.

4. **Overwhelming the Reader**: Long, overly technical reports without a clear structure can confuse readers. Use headings, concise language, and summaries to improve readability.

5. **Inconsistent Severity Ratings**: Arbitrary or inconsistent severity ratings can mislead stakeholders about which issues need immediate attention.

A well-crafted vulnerability report is essential for communicating the results of a penetration test and helping clients understand and address their security weaknesses. By focusing on clear descriptions, evidence-backed findings, and actionable recommendations, ethical hackers can ensure their reports are both informative and effective.

In the next chapter, we'll discuss incident response and post-attack remediation. This phase involves steps that organizations take to respond to and recover from security incidents, leveraging the findings from penetration tests to improve overall resilience and prevent future breaches.

CHAPTER 19: POST-EXPLOITATION AND COVERING TRACKS

In penetration testing, post-exploitation refers to the actions taken after gaining initial access to a system. The goal of this phase is to assess the extent of access, gather valuable information, maintain persistence, and explore how an attacker might advance further within the network. Covering tracks involves taking steps to ensure that these activities remain undetected. While these techniques mimic real-world attacker behavior, they should only be practiced in controlled and authorized simulations.

In this chapter, we'll discuss techniques for maintaining access, establishing persistence, and covering tracks, and we'll explore why stealth techniques are limited to authorized environments.

Post-Exploitation Goals and Techniques

Once ethical hackers have gained access to a system, the post-exploitation phase helps them assess the potential impact of the breach, including the level of access, sensitive information exposure, and possible paths for lateral movement within the network.

Key Goals in Post-Exploitation

1. **Privilege Escalation**: Attempting to elevate permissions, such as moving from a regular user account to an administrative or root level, to increase the scope of accessible resources.

2. **Data Collection**: Gathering information that may be valuable, such as credentials, configuration files, databases, or sensitive files.

3. **Lateral Movement**: Expanding access to other systems within the network to simulate an attacker's path toward high-value targets.

4. **Persistence**: Setting up mechanisms to retain access, even if the initial exploit is patched or the system is rebooted.

Maintaining Access and Persistence Techniques

Maintaining access ensures that penetration testers can return to the system even if they lose their initial entry point. Persistence is often achieved by setting up additional access points or embedding "backdoors" in authorized simulations. Ethical hackers use these techniques with caution, as persistence can interfere with regular operations if not removed post-testing.

1. Backdoors

A backdoor is a hidden entry point that provides continuous access to the system. Attackers might use custom scripts, modified configurations, or hidden accounts to set up backdoors.

- **Example**: Adding a user account with high privileges, hidden from regular user lists, to regain access if needed.

- **Caution**: Ethical hackers must remove any backdoors created during testing to prevent unauthorized access post-test.

2. Scheduled Tasks (Windows) or Cron Jobs (Linux)

Scheduled tasks on Windows and cron jobs on Linux can execute scripts or commands at specified times or intervals, maintaining access or triggering specific actions.

- **Example**: Creating a scheduled task to start a reverse shell every 24 hours, allowing the tester to reconnect if access is lost.

- **Caution**: These tasks must be set to expire or be deleted after testing to avoid impacting system functionality.

3. Modifying Startup Scripts

Startup scripts execute commands automatically when the system boots, making them an effective persistence technique.

- **Example**: Adding a command to a startup script that opens a reverse shell on boot, reconnecting the tester to the target system.

- **Caution**: Modifying startup scripts may create system instability if not properly removed.

4. Registry Changes

In Windows systems, modifying registry entries can enable persistence by setting applications or scripts to run at startup.

- **Example**: Editing registry keys to launch a hidden process upon login, allowing the tester to regain access each time the system restarts.

- **Caution**: Registry modifications can interfere with system behavior and should be limited to authorized test environments.

5. Planting Web Shells

In web applications, a web shell is a script that provides remote access via the web server. This allows the tester to issue commands and interact with the server through a web interface.

- **Example**: Uploading a PHP web shell to a vulnerable website, which can be accessed via a hidden URL to execute commands on the server.

- **Caution**: Web shells should only be used in testing environments, as they create significant security risks if left in production systems.

Covering Tracks: Stealth Techniques

Covering tracks involves hiding evidence of an attacker's presence, such as clearing logs or deleting temporary files created during exploitation. While real attackers cover their tracks to evade detection, ethical hackers must take extreme care when performing these activities, as they can impact system integrity and complicate incident response.

Common Techniques for Covering Tracks

1. Log Clearing

Attackers often clear system and event logs to erase traces of their actions. Ethical hackers may practice this technique in simulated environments to understand how attackers erase evidence.

- **Example**: Using commands like Clear-EventLog on Windows or deleting specific log files on Linux, such as /var/log/auth.log.

- **Caution**: Log clearing should only be done in test environments, as it removes valuable information that security teams need for auditing and incident response.

2. File and Process Hiding

Attackers may disguise or hide files and processes to avoid detection. This is often done by renaming files, moving them to hidden directories, or using rootkit software to mask malicious processes.

- **Example**: Renaming a malicious script to resemble a legitimate system file or placing it in an obscure directory.

- **Caution**: Altering files and processes can destabilize systems if not reverted after testing.

3. **Disabling Security Software**

Attackers often attempt to disable antivirus software or intrusion detection systems (IDS) to avoid detection. Ethical hackers may test this in simulations to understand how security software responds.

- **Example**: Using commands to disable security services or kill monitoring processes.

- **Caution**: Disabling security software is highly disruptive and should only be done in lab environments.

4. **Removing Artifacts**

Artifacts, such as temporary files, scripts, and modified configurations, are often left behind by attackers. Ethical hackers may delete these to simulate how attackers erase evidence of their activities.

- **Example**: Removing uploaded files, clearing temporary directories, or undoing configuration changes made during exploitation.

- **Caution**: Removing artifacts should be carefully documented and performed only in authorized environments to avoid disrupting normal operations.

5. Network Obfuscation

Network obfuscation techniques help attackers disguise their IP addresses or route their traffic through multiple systems to avoid detection.

- **Example**: Using proxies, VPNs, or TOR to mask the origin of network traffic.

- **Caution**: Ethical hackers must comply with the organization's network policies and limit network obfuscation to avoid interfering with legitimate traffic.

Why Covering Tracks Should Only Be Practiced in Authorized Simulations

While understanding stealth techniques is valuable for ethical hackers, covering tracks in a live environment without clear authorization can lead to serious issues, including:

- **Data Loss**: Clearing logs or deleting artifacts can erase valuable information, hindering incident response and forensic analysis.

- **System Instability**: Modifying files, configurations, or security settings can destabilize the system, creating service disruptions or unexpected behavior.

- **Compromised Audits**: Altering or hiding logs interferes with security audits, making it difficult for organizations to track activity and assess security.

- **Legal Consequences**: Unauthorized actions, such as disabling security software or deleting logs, may breach regulatory compliance and lead to legal repercussions.

In penetration testing, ethical hackers prioritize transparency and maintain detailed records of all activities to ensure accountability. Covering tracks is generally limited to authorized simulations, where these actions are carefully monitored and documented for educational or research purposes.

Example: Post-Exploitation Scenario

Here's a scenario to illustrate how post-exploitation and covering tracks might be handled in a controlled environment.

Scenario: Maintaining Access and Covering Tracks in a Test Environment

1. **Objective**: The ethical hacker has gained low-level access to a web server in a test environment and aims to escalate privileges and establish persistence.

2. **Privilege Escalation**: The hacker finds a misconfigured sudo permission, allowing them to gain root access.

3. **Establishing Persistence**:

   ○ They add a cron job that runs a script every hour, creating a reverse shell connection.

4. **Covering Tracks**:

   ○ The hacker deletes the initial script used to establish access.

   ○ They remove entries from the command history file and clear the cron log entries associated with the persistence task.

Caution: These actions are documented in a detailed test report and are carefully controlled. After testing, all changes are reverted, and the environment is restored to its original state.

Best Practices for Ethical Post-Exploitation and Covering Tracks

Ethical hackers should adhere to the following best practices during post-exploitation testing:

1. **Document Every Action**: Keep detailed records of each command, configuration change, and script used, allowing the organization to fully understand the impact and easily revert changes.

2. **Limit Persistence Methods**: Use the minimum level of persistence necessary and ensure all mechanisms are removed after testing.

3. **Avoid Modifying Production Logs**: Use separate logging mechanisms to record activities rather than clearing or tampering with production logs.

4. **Simulate Stealth Tactics in Sandboxed Environments**: Perform log clearing, file hiding, and process masking only in isolated lab environments, where they won't impact operational systems.

5. **Communicate Transparently**: Ensure all post-exploitation activities align with the client's expectations, and notify the organization if any potential issues arise.

Ethical and Legal Considerations in Post-Exploitation Testing

Ethical hackers must conduct post-exploitation and track-covering exercises responsibly, ensuring they align with legal and ethical standards:

- **Obtain Written Consent**: Explicit authorization is required for any post-exploitation or track-covering activities.

- **Respect Organizational Policies**: Follow the organization's security policies, and avoid actions that may interfere with compliance or regulatory requirements.

- **Report All Persistence Mechanisms**: Document every backdoor, cron job, or scheduled task created during testing and remove them upon completion.

- **Limit Data Access**: Avoid accessing sensitive data or confidential files unless specifically authorized by the organization.

A comprehensive post-exploitation report includes clear documentation of all actions taken, allowing the organization to review, verify, and revert any changes made during testing.

Post-exploitation and covering tracks are advanced phases of penetration testing that provide insights into how attackers maintain access and avoid detection. While these techniques are valuable for understanding attacker behavior, they require strict ethical guidelines, clear documentation, and should only be performed in authorized, controlled environments.

In the next chapter, we'll delve into incident response and remediation, focusing on how organizations can respond to security incidents, contain threats, and recover from attacks. Understanding incident response helps ethical hackers better support clients in enhancing their overall resilience against cybersecurity threats.

CHAPTER 20: ETHICAL HACKING TOOLS AND FRAMEWORKS

In ethical hacking, tools and frameworks are essential for conducting thorough assessments. From scanning and reconnaissance to exploitation and reporting, each tool serves a specific purpose within the penetration testing process. In this chapter, we'll provide an overview of popular tools like Metasploit, Nmap, and Burp Suite, detailing how each fits into an ethical hacker's toolkit and the phases of penetration testing they support.

Understanding Ethical Hacking Tools and Frameworks

Ethical hacking tools are software applications or platforms that help penetration testers simulate attacks, identify vulnerabilities, and assess system defenses. Many tools are open-source or community-supported, providing flexibility and allowing customization to suit specific testing needs. Frameworks, on the other hand, are structured methodologies that outline best practices, stages, and guidelines for conducting penetration tests.

Key Ethical Hacking Tools

Here's a look at some of the most widely used ethical hacking tools and how they contribute to various phases of penetration testing.

1. Nmap (Network Mapper)

- **Category**: Network Scanning and Enumeration

- **Purpose**: Nmap is a powerful open-source tool for network discovery and security auditing. It's commonly used to scan networks, discover active hosts, open ports, and services, and gather information about the network structure.

- **Key Features**:

  o **Port Scanning**: Identifies open ports and running services on a network.

  o **Service and Version Detection**: Determines the version of software running on each open port.

  o **OS Detection**: Infers the operating system of scanned devices.

  o **Scriptable**: Nmap's scripting engine (NSE) allows custom scripts for vulnerability detection.

- **Common Use Cases**:

  o Initial reconnaissance and mapping network structure.

  o Identifying services that may be vulnerable to specific attacks.

Example Command:

bash

nmap -sV -O -Pn [target IP]

This command performs a version scan (-sV), OS detection (-O), and disables host discovery (-Pn), scanning the specified IP address.

2. Metasploit Framework

- **Category**: Exploitation and Post-Exploitation

- **Purpose**: Metasploit is an open-source penetration testing platform that includes numerous pre-built exploits, payloads, and auxiliary modules. It allows ethical hackers to identify vulnerabilities, gain access, and simulate various types of attacks.

- **Key Features**:

  o **Exploit Database**: Contains a large library of exploits for known vulnerabilities.

  o **Payloads**: Customizable payloads for remote access, data exfiltration, and privilege escalation.

  o **Auxiliary Modules**: Scanning, reconnaissance, and brute-forcing modules.

  o **Post-Exploitation**: Tools for maintaining access, extracting information, and testing persistence.

- **Common Use Cases**:

o Exploiting vulnerable services and verifying the impact of vulnerabilities.

o Conducting controlled post-exploitation activities for demonstration purposes.

Example Command:

bash

msfconsole

use exploit/windows/smb/ms17_010_eternalblue

set RHOST [target IP]

exploit

This command runs Metasploit's msfconsole, loads the EternalBlue exploit module for SMB, and launches the exploit against the target IP.

3. Burp Suite

- **Category**: Web Application Testing

- **Purpose**: Burp Suite is a comprehensive platform for testing web application security. It provides tools for intercepting, analyzing, and manipulating HTTP requests, making it essential for testing vulnerabilities like SQL injection, XSS, and CSRF.

- **Key Features**:

  - **Proxy**: Intercepts and analyzes HTTP requests and responses.

  - **Spidering**: Maps web applications and finds hidden pages or directories.

  - **Intruder**: Automates attacks by brute-forcing input fields.

  - **Scanner**: Automatically detects common web vulnerabilities.

- **Common Use Cases**:

  - Testing web applications for vulnerabilities like SQL injection, XSS, and CSRF.

  - Capturing and analyzing traffic to understand how applications handle data.

Example:

- Configure Burp Suite to intercept HTTP requests from a browser. Modify request parameters to test for SQL injection vulnerabilities, then use Intruder to automate payload testing.

4. Wireshark

- **Category**: Network Traffic Analysis

- **Purpose**: Wireshark is an open-source packet analyzer that allows ethical hackers to capture, analyze, and inspect network traffic in detail. It's often used to detect data leaks, understand communication protocols, and identify abnormal traffic.

- **Key Features**:

    o **Real-Time Packet Capture**: Records all network traffic across various protocols.

    o **Filtering and Analysis**: Allows detailed filtering of captured data for targeted analysis.

    o **Protocol Dissection**: Breaks down packet contents by protocol, showing source, destination, and data.

- **Common Use Cases**:

    o Analyzing suspicious traffic, detecting plain text data transmission, and identifying potential data exfiltration.

Example Command:

- Capture HTTP traffic by setting http as the filter in Wireshark to monitor unencrypted data transmissions.

5. John the Ripper

- **Category**: Password Cracking

- **Purpose**: John the Ripper is a popular open-source password cracking tool. It uses dictionary attacks, brute force, and custom wordlists to crack password hashes, commonly used in post-exploitation for testing weak passwords.

- **Key Features**:

  o **Dictionary Attacks**: Uses a list of commonly used passwords to crack hashes.

  o **Brute Force Attacks**: Tests all possible combinations of characters.

  o **Customizable Wordlists**: Supports custom wordlists for targeted password cracking.

- **Common Use Cases**:

  o Testing the strength of hashed passwords obtained through privilege escalation.

  o Simulating brute-force attacks to demonstrate the risk of weak passwords.

Example Command:

bash

john --wordlist=/path/to/wordlist.txt hashfile.txt

This command uses John the Ripper to attempt cracking the hashes in hashfile.txt using a specified wordlist.

Supporting Tools in the Ethical Hacker's Toolkit

While the above tools are commonly used, ethical hackers may also rely on additional tools to support various phases of penetration testing:

1. **Hydra** – A fast network login brute-forcing tool used to test weak credentials on services like SSH, FTP, and HTTP.

2. **Nessus** – A vulnerability scanner that detects common software vulnerabilities, configuration issues, and missing patches. Nessus provides detailed reports on each vulnerability it detects.

3. **Cuckoo Sandbox** – A malware analysis tool that allows ethical hackers to execute suspicious files in an isolated environment, monitoring their behavior without risk to the main system.

4. **Nikto** – A web server scanner that checks for outdated software, default configurations, and other potential security issues.

5. **OpenVAS** – An open-source vulnerability assessment scanner used to detect and report vulnerabilities across various operating systems and applications.

6. **Aircrack-ng** – A suite of tools for auditing Wi-Fi network security, allowing ethical hackers to capture packets, analyze network traffic, and test WPA/WPA2-PSK passwords.

How Each Tool Fits into the Ethical Hacking Process

Ethical hacking tools support specific phases within the structured penetration testing process. Here's a breakdown of where each tool is typically used:

1. **Reconnaissance (Planning and Information Gathering)**

   o **Tools**: Nmap, Nikto, OpenVAS

   o **Purpose**: Gathering information about open ports, services, and configurations.

2. **Scanning and Enumeration**

   o **Tools**: Nmap, Nessus, OpenVAS

   o **Purpose**: Identifying vulnerabilities in network services, applications, and operating systems.

3. **Exploitation**

   o **Tools**: Metasploit, Burp Suite, Hydra, Aircrack-ng

   o **Purpose**: Using identified vulnerabilities to gain access, test credential strength, or exploit network weaknesses.

4. **Post-Exploitation and Persistence**

   o **Tools**: Metasploit, John the Ripper

   o **Purpose**: Escalating privileges, extracting sensitive data, and establishing persistence for testing.

5. **Traffic Analysis and Network Monitoring**

   o **Tools**: Wireshark, Cuckoo Sandbox

   o **Purpose**: Monitoring traffic, detecting suspicious patterns, and analyzing potential data exfiltration.

6. **Reporting and Documentation**

   o **Purpose**: While reporting tools aren't typically included in these stages, some platforms (e.g., Nessus) generate reports to streamline documentation.

Ethical Considerations for Tool Usage

Ethical hackers must use these tools responsibly, following strict ethical and legal guidelines:

1. **Authorization**: Only use tools on networks and systems with explicit permission to avoid unauthorized access and legal repercussions.

2. **Limited Scope**: Use tools within the agreed scope and avoid probing external systems or networks outside the target environment.

3. **Transparency and Documentation**: Document each tool used and its purpose to ensure transparency and accountability during testing.

4. **Respect Data Privacy**: Avoid capturing sensitive data, and restrict the use of tools that may impact the privacy of non-targeted users.

Best Practices for Effective Tool Usage

To maximize the effectiveness of these tools, ethical hackers should follow these best practices:

1. **Understand Each Tool's Capabilities**: Familiarize yourself with each tool's features, limitations, and appropriate use cases to use them effectively.

2. **Combine Tools for Comprehensive Testing**: No single tool provides complete coverage. Use multiple tools to cross-verify findings and ensure thorough testing.

3. **Customize Tool Settings**: Adjust tool configurations and scripts to match the specific requirements of each test, ensuring accurate and relevant results.

4. **Stay Updated on Tool Development**: Ethical hacking tools are regularly updated with new features, modules, and vulnerability data. Keep tools updated to ensure they cover the latest vulnerabilities.

5. **Practice in Lab Environments**: Before using tools on a client network, practice in lab environments to refine techniques and understand each tool's impact.

Tools and frameworks are essential components of an ethical hacker's toolkit, providing the resources needed to conduct effective penetration testing. From Nmap's reconnaissance capabilities to Metasploit's exploitation features and Burp Suite's web application analysis, each tool plays a unique role in identifying and mitigating security risks. However, with great power comes responsibility; ethical hackers must use these tools within authorized environments and adhere to best practices to ensure ethical and legal compliance.

In the next chapter, we'll discuss incident response and remediation, examining how organizations can respond to security incidents and recover from attacks. Incident response is critical for minimizing the impact of security events and protecting organizations against future threats.

CHAPTER 21: CASE STUDIES AND REAL-WORLD APPLICATIONS

Ethical hacking has played a vital role in securing organizations worldwide, preventing potentially catastrophic breaches and raising awareness about cybersecurity practices. In this chapter, we'll analyze famous ethical hacking cases, examining how penetration tests and vulnerability assessments uncovered significant security flaws. Each case study provides valuable lessons on the importance of ethical hacking and demonstrates how proactive security measures have saved companies from data breaches and financial loss.

Case Study 1: The Google Vulnerability Rewards Program (VRP)

Background: In 2010, Google launched one of the first large-scale vulnerability rewards programs (VRP) for web applications. Google invited ethical hackers to report security flaws in its services, offering monetary rewards based on the severity of the vulnerabilities discovered. This program aimed to enhance Google's security by leveraging the skills of ethical hackers worldwide.

Key Findings and Impact

- **Cross-Site Scripting (XSS) and SQL Injection**: Ethical hackers discovered critical XSS and SQL injection vulnerabilities in various Google services, including Gmail and Google Docs, which, if exploited, could have led to data theft and account compromise.

- **Authentication Flaws**: In 2014, an ethical hacker discovered a bug that allowed unauthorized access to Google services, risking exposure of sensitive user data.

- **Subdomain Takeovers**: Ethical hackers found that some abandoned or misconfigured subdomains could be taken over by attackers. These vulnerabilities would have allowed attackers to host malicious content under a legitimate Google URL.

Lessons Learned:

- **Value of Crowdsourced Testing**: By incentivizing ethical hackers worldwide, Google expanded its security testing capabilities far beyond its internal team's resources.

- **Proactive Security**: By addressing vulnerabilities before they were exploited, Google prevented potential breaches, setting an industry standard for VRPs.

- **Regular Testing**: Ongoing vulnerability rewards programs ensure continuous improvement, as new vulnerabilities arise with updates to applications and infrastructure.

Outcome: Google's VRP helped establish a global trend for vulnerability rewards programs, with major companies like Facebook, Apple, and Microsoft adopting similar approaches.

Case Study 2: The Facebook Login Flaw

Background: In 2018, an ethical hacker named Anand Prakash discovered a critical vulnerability in Facebook's account recovery system. This vulnerability allowed an attacker to brute-force Facebook's password reset feature and gain unauthorized access to any Facebook account.

Key Findings and Impact

- **Vulnerability Description**: When a user forgot their password, Facebook's account recovery system sent a six-digit verification code via email or SMS. However, there were no rate limits on attempts to enter this code, allowing attackers to brute-force all possible combinations (1,000,000 possibilities) in a relatively short period.

- **Potential Impact**: If exploited, attackers could have accessed personal data, messages, and photos in any Facebook account, leading to identity theft, social engineering attacks, and loss of privacy for millions of users.

Lessons Learned:

- **Importance of Rate Limiting**: Implementing rate limits on sensitive actions like password resets can prevent brute-force attacks.

- **Testing All Access Points**: Even non-traditional entry points (such as account recovery and password reset) need to be tested for vulnerabilities.

- **Value of Bug Bounties**: Facebook's Bug Bounty program incentivized ethical hackers to find vulnerabilities, which allowed the company to fix this issue before it could be exploited.

Outcome: Facebook rewarded Prakash with a $15,000 bounty, and the vulnerability was patched immediately. This case underscores the importance of rigorous testing of all account management processes.

Case Study 3: Uber's AWS S3 Bucket Exposure

Background: In 2016, ethical hackers discovered a misconfigured Amazon S3 bucket (a cloud storage repository) in Uber's cloud environment. The bucket contained sensitive information, including customer and driver data. This discovery revealed a critical security oversight in Uber's cloud configuration.

Key Findings and Impact

- **Data Exposure**: The exposed S3 bucket contained confidential information, including private customer and driver details, such as names, addresses, and driver's license numbers.

- **Configuration Flaw**: The S3 bucket had incorrect permissions, allowing public access to files that should have been private. This oversight highlighted the risks associated with cloud storage misconfigurations.

- **Incident Response Delay**: Uber initially failed to disclose the breach, which led to public backlash and regulatory scrutiny.

Lessons Learned:

- **Cloud Security Awareness**: Organizations must apply strict access controls to cloud storage and use automated tools to detect misconfigurations.

- **Proactive Auditing**: Regular audits of cloud storage configurations can prevent accidental exposure of sensitive data.

- **Transparent Incident Response**: Organizations should promptly address and disclose security incidents to maintain trust and comply with regulatory requirements.

Outcome: This incident led Uber to improve its cloud security protocols and transparency practices. The company now conducts regular security assessments and uses automated tools to monitor for misconfigurations in its cloud infrastructure.

Case Study 4: Marriott's Data Breach Prevention

Background: In 2019, Marriott International engaged ethical hackers to conduct a penetration test on their systems. During testing, they identified several vulnerabilities in Marriott's network that could have led to data breaches similar to an earlier breach in 2018 that affected up to 500 million guests.

Key Findings and Impact

- **Vulnerability Detection**: The penetration test revealed unpatched software and misconfigured access controls in Marriott's network infrastructure.

- **Sensitive Data Access**: Ethical hackers discovered that some systems with customer data were accessible with insufficient authentication, exposing personal information.

- **Improvement of Access Controls**: The test prompted Marriott to implement multi-factor authentication (MFA) and review access privileges, enhancing data security.

Lessons Learned:

- **Post-Incident Proactive Testing**: After a breach, it's essential to perform rigorous penetration tests to identify and fix remaining vulnerabilities.

- **Importance of Access Controls**: Strong authentication and access control policies are critical to protecting sensitive data, particularly for large organizations with distributed networks.

- **Regular Patch Management**: Ensuring that software is up to date prevents attackers from exploiting known vulnerabilities.

Outcome: The penetration test helped Marriott avoid further breaches by addressing vulnerabilities proactively. It reinforced the company's commitment to data security, leading to enhanced security policies and regular testing.

Case Study 5: Capital One's Insider Threat Detection

Background: In 2020, ethical hackers helped Capital One improve its detection of insider threats. This assessment was prompted by a previous breach where an insider accessed an improperly configured Amazon Web Services (AWS) environment and exfiltrated customer data.

Key Findings and Impact

- **Insider Access Controls**: Ethical hackers identified weaknesses in Capital One's policies for internal access, noting that certain employees had excessive permissions to sensitive cloud resources.

- **Logging and Monitoring Improvements**: The assessment revealed insufficient monitoring of employee activities on cloud systems, limiting the company's ability to detect suspicious behavior.

- **Cloud Security Hardening**: The test led to improved configurations in Capital One's AWS environment, including enhanced IAM (Identity and Access Management) policies.

Lessons Learned:

- **Insider Threat Awareness**: Companies must implement strict internal access policies, limiting permissions to essential users only.

- **Continuous Monitoring**: Implementing real-time monitoring of employee actions and access to sensitive resources is critical for early detection of insider threats.

- **Regular Cloud Audits**: Performing cloud security audits helps prevent misconfigurations that could be exploited by insiders or external attackers.

Outcome: The ethical hacking engagement helped Capital One implement stronger access controls and proactive monitoring, reducing the risk of future insider threats. The company's commitment to cloud security improvements has since become a model in the financial industry.

Lessons Learned from Ethical Hacking Case Studies

Across these case studies, we see common themes and lessons that can help organizations strengthen their security posture:

1. **Value of Bug Bounty Programs and VRPs**: Crowdsourced testing enables organizations to tap into a wide pool of skilled ethical hackers who can uncover vulnerabilities at scale. Programs like those run by Google and Facebook have helped prevent major security incidents by addressing flaws before attackers could exploit them.

2. **Importance of Access Control and Authentication**: Implementing access control measures, such as multi-factor authentication and least-privilege access, is essential for protecting sensitive systems and data, as shown in cases involving Marriott and Capital One.

3. **Cloud Security and Configuration Management**: Misconfigured cloud resources, like Amazon S3 buckets, are common attack vectors. Regular audits, automated monitoring, and strict access controls are necessary to secure cloud environments, as seen in the Uber and Capital One incidents.

4. **Proactive Vulnerability Management**: Regular vulnerability assessments and penetration tests help organizations stay ahead of evolving threats. Organizations like Marriott that proactively tested their security postures after incidents were better positioned to prevent future breaches.

5. **Transparency and Responsible Incident Response**: Transparent communication about security incidents builds trust with customers and regulatory bodies. Organizations should respond swiftly and transparently to security breaches, as delays can lead to reputational damage, as observed with Uber's initial handling of its cloud data exposure.

These real-world ethical hacking cases underscore the importance of proactive security measures, regular vulnerability assessments, and thorough testing of systems. By analyzing these cases, organizations can learn valuable lessons in preventing data breaches, managing insider threats, and ensuring secure cloud configurations.

Ethical hacking continues to play a crucial role in the cybersecurity landscape, helping companies strengthen defenses, protect user data, and maintain trust with their customers.

In the next chapter, we'll discuss the future of ethical hacking and emerging trends in cybersecurity. We'll explore how evolving technologies, such as artificial intelligence and machine learning, are shaping the field and creating new challenges and opportunities for ethical hackers.

CHAPTER 22: BUILDING A CAREER IN ETHICAL HACKING

With the increasing demand for cybersecurity professionals, ethical hacking offers a rewarding career path that combines problem-solving skills with technical expertise. This chapter provides guidance on certifications, skill-building strategies, and tips for securing a position in ethical hacking. We'll also cover pathways for continuous learning and professional development to help aspiring ethical hackers stay ahead in this dynamic field.

Getting Started in Ethical Hacking

Starting a career in ethical hacking requires a mix of foundational skills, formal training, and hands-on experience. Here are the core steps to take if you're beginning your journey:

1. **Build a Strong Foundation in IT**: A good understanding of networking, operating systems, and programming is essential. Familiarity with concepts such as TCP/IP, routing, DNS, Linux, Windows administration, and programming languages (e.g., Python, Bash scripting) is crucial for ethical hacking.

2. **Learn Cybersecurity Basics**: Before diving into offensive security, gain an understanding of cybersecurity fundamentals, including risk management, security controls, and defensive security measures. Platforms like

Cybersecurity Fundamentals on Khan Academy can be a great starting point.

3. **Practice Hands-On Skills**: Ethical hacking requires practical experience with real-world scenarios. Platforms like TryHackMe, Hack The Box, and OverTheWire offer hands-on labs and challenges that simulate security vulnerabilities and allow you to practice penetration testing techniques.

Essential Certifications for Ethical Hackers

Certifications provide credibility and help demonstrate your skills to potential employers. Here are some of the most recognized certifications in ethical hacking and cybersecurity:

1. **Certified Ethical Hacker (CEH)**

    o **Overview**: The CEH certification, offered by EC-Council, is one of the most recognized entry-level certifications for ethical hackers. It covers a broad range of topics, including network scanning, vulnerability assessment, social engineering, and malware analysis.

    o **Recommended For**: Beginners looking to establish credibility in ethical hacking.

o **Skills Gained**: Fundamentals of hacking techniques and tools, as well as the phases of a penetration test.

2. **CompTIA Security+**

   o **Overview**: CompTIA Security+ is a general cybersecurity certification that provides a strong foundation in security concepts, risk management, cryptography, and identity management.

   o **Recommended For**: Those new to cybersecurity who want a solid understanding of the field.

   o **Skills Gained**: Basic cybersecurity knowledge, which is valuable for building a foundation before pursuing more specialized certifications.

3. **Offensive Security Certified Professional (OSCP)**

   o **Overview**: Offered by Offensive Security, OSCP is a highly respected, hands-on certification focusing on penetration testing and offensive security skills. The OSCP exam requires candidates to exploit vulnerabilities in a controlled lab environment, demonstrating real-world hacking skills.

   o **Recommended For**: Intermediate and advanced practitioners with hands-on experience.

- o **Skills Gained**: Exploitation techniques, network and system penetration testing, post-exploitation skills, and reporting.

4. **GIAC Penetration Tester (GPEN)**

- o **Overview**: Provided by the Global Information Assurance Certification (GIAC), GPEN covers various penetration testing methodologies and tools, focusing on in-depth analysis of network and web vulnerabilities.

- o **Recommended For**: Intermediate practitioners who want a well-rounded certification that's respected in the industry.

- o **Skills Gained**: Network reconnaissance, exploitation techniques, and detailed reporting skills.

5. **Certified Information Systems Security Professional (CISSP)**

- o **Overview**: CISSP is a comprehensive certification that covers multiple domains of cybersecurity. Although not exclusively focused on ethical hacking, it's highly valued for those seeking senior roles in cybersecurity.

- **Recommended For**: Advanced practitioners with at least five years of experience in cybersecurity.

- **Skills Gained**: Broad understanding of security principles, including risk management, asset security, and software development security.

Additional Certifications:

- **Certified Information Security Manager (CISM)**: Useful for those interested in management roles.

- **Certified Cloud Security Professional (CCSP)**: Focused on cloud security, ideal for roles involving cloud environments.

Developing Essential Skills for Ethical Hacking

Ethical hackers need a unique blend of technical skills and problem-solving abilities. Here are some key skills to focus on:

1. **Programming and Scripting**: Familiarity with languages like Python, Bash, and PowerShell is essential for writing custom scripts, automating tasks, and creating exploits.

2. **Networking**: Understanding network protocols, packet analysis, and network security measures is fundamental. Knowledge of TCP/IP, subnetting, firewalls, VPNs, and wireless security is crucial for penetration testing.

3. **Operating Systems**:

   o **Linux**: Many hacking tools are designed for Linux. Kali Linux, a distribution tailored for penetration testing, is widely used in the field.

   o **Windows**: Since many corporate environments use Windows, familiarity with Windows security features, Active Directory, and PowerShell is essential.

4. **Web Application Security**: With web applications as primary targets, understanding web security concepts like SQL injection, cross-site scripting (XSS), and CSRF is critical.

5. **Reverse Engineering and Malware Analysis**: Familiarity with reverse engineering tools, assembly language, and malware analysis helps identify and neutralize malicious software.

6. **Soft Skills**: Communication, report writing, and analytical skills are essential for translating technical findings into actionable insights for stakeholders. Ethical hackers need to explain their findings clearly to technical and non-technical audiences alike.

Finding Job Opportunities in Ethical Hacking

Ethical hacking roles can vary depending on industry and organization size. Here are some common job titles and tips for finding a position in the field:

Job Titles for Ethical Hackers

1. **Penetration Tester**: Performs controlled attacks on systems and networks to identify vulnerabilities. Often requires strong technical skills and certifications like OSCP.

2. **Security Analyst**: Monitors and analyzes security events, often working within Security Operations Centers (SOCs) to detect and respond to threats.

3. **Red Team Member**: Part of a team that conducts full-scale attack simulations, often for larger organizations. Red teamers typically perform more sophisticated and persistent attacks.

4. **Vulnerability Assessment Analyst**: Focuses on scanning and identifying vulnerabilities, often using automated tools like Nessus and OpenVAS.

5. **Application Security Engineer**: Ensures the security of web and mobile applications, performing code reviews, penetration tests, and vulnerability assessments.

6. **Security Consultant**: Works as an independent or contracted professional, conducting security assessments, advising clients, and helping to implement security solutions.

Tips for Landing a Job in Ethical Hacking

1. **Gain Practical Experience**: Build a portfolio by solving challenges on platforms like Hack The Box, TryHackMe, or CTF competitions. Share your solutions and projects on platforms like GitHub or a personal blog to showcase your skills.

2. **Build a Strong Online Presence**: Follow cybersecurity blogs, engage in forums, and contribute to open-source security projects. Having a professional online presence on LinkedIn or GitHub can attract potential employers.

3. **Network and Attend Industry Events**: Cybersecurity conferences like DEF CON, Black Hat, and BSides offer networking opportunities and allow you to learn from experienced professionals. Joining local cybersecurity meetups can also help build connections.

4. **Apply for Internships and Entry-Level Roles**: Starting with an internship or a junior security role, like a Security Analyst, can help you gain experience and build a foundation for an ethical hacking career.

5. **Stay Updated on Industry Trends**: Cybersecurity is constantly evolving, so staying informed about the latest vulnerabilities, attack methods, and security tools is essential. Subscribe to cybersecurity newsletters, join online communities, and follow thought leaders in the field.

Pathways for Further Learning and Professional Development

Ethical hacking is a field that requires continuous learning and adaptation. Here are ways to stay current and deepen your expertise:

1. **Advanced Certifications and Specializations**:

   o Pursue advanced certifications like **OSCE (Offensive Security Certified Expert)**, focusing on advanced exploitation techniques, or **CISSP** for managerial roles.

   o Explore specialization certifications, such as **Certified Cloud Security Professional (CCSP)** for cloud security or **GIAC Web Application Penetration Tester (GWAPT)** for web security.

2. **Contribute to Open-Source Projects**:

   o Participating in open-source security projects allows you to gain experience, learn from others, and showcase your contributions. Popular platforms include GitHub and GitLab.

3. **Research and Write about Security Topics**:

   o Start a blog, publish research papers, or contribute to cybersecurity publications. Writing about complex topics improves your understanding and builds credibility in the field.

4. **Join Capture the Flag (CTF) Competitions**:

   o CTF competitions offer hands-on practice in ethical hacking, from binary exploitation to web challenges. These competitions improve skills, build your resume, and connect you with the ethical hacking community.

5. **Learn About New Technologies**:

   o Explore emerging technologies, such as **cloud security**, **IoT security**, and **machine learning**. As organizations adopt these technologies, understanding their security implications will make you a more versatile ethical hacker.

6. **Engage in Bug Bounty Programs**:

   o Platforms like HackerOne, Bugcrowd, and Synack provide real-world hacking opportunities by allowing ethical hackers to find vulnerabilities in live applications and earn rewards. Bug bounty programs offer hands-on experience, and successful reports can build your reputation.

7. **Stay Informed on Emerging Trends**:

   o Keep up with trends in cybersecurity, such as the rise of artificial intelligence, quantum computing threats, and advancements in cybersecurity automation. Following industry news and participating in webinars or workshops can help you stay ahead.

Building a career in ethical hacking requires a combination of foundational knowledge, hands-on experience, and continuous learning. With the right certifications, technical skills, and a proactive approach to professional development, ethical hackers can secure rewarding roles in cybersecurity and contribute to a safer digital landscape.

Whether you're just starting or looking to advance your career, ethical hacking offers exciting and impactful opportunities. By focusing on skill-building, networking, and staying updated with emerging trends, you can develop a successful and fulfilling career in this dynamic field.

This concludes our journey through ethical hacking. Remember, the most successful ethical hackers are those who stay curious, continue learning, and maintain a strong commitment to ethical principles.